GLOUCESTER MASSACHUSETTS

1000

GREETINGS

ROCKPORT PUBLISHERS

creative correspondence designed for all occasions   PETER KING & COMPANY

First published in the United States of America by
Rockport Publishers, Inc.
33 Commercial Street
Gloucester, Massachusetts 01930-5089
Telephone: (978) 282-9590
Fax: (978) 283-2742
www.rockpub.com

Library of Congress Cataloging-in-Publication Data
King, Peter.
  1,000 greetings : creative correspondence designed for all occasions / Peter King &
Co.
     p.   cm.
  ISBN 1-59253-021-4 (flexibind)
  1. Greeting cards—Design—Catalogs. I. Title: One thousand greetings. II. Title.
NC1860.K55 2004
741.6'84—dc22   2003023356
                                                             CIP

ISBN 1-59253-021-4

10 9 8 7

Design: Peter King & Company
Cover Image: Bobbie Bush Photography, bobbie@bobbiebush.com

Printed in China

THANKS TO THE MANY WHOSE INSPIRING CREATIVITY AND DILIGENCE MADE THIS BOOK POSSIBLE.

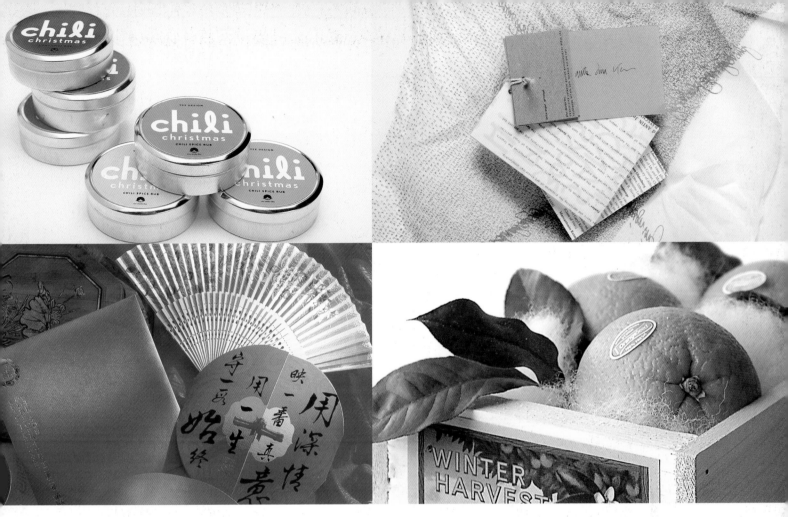

CONTENTS

GREETINGS

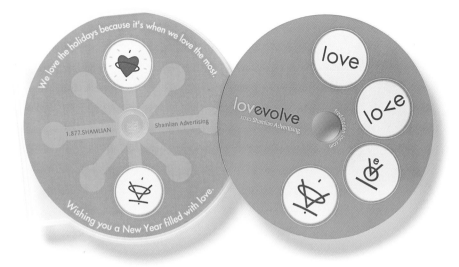

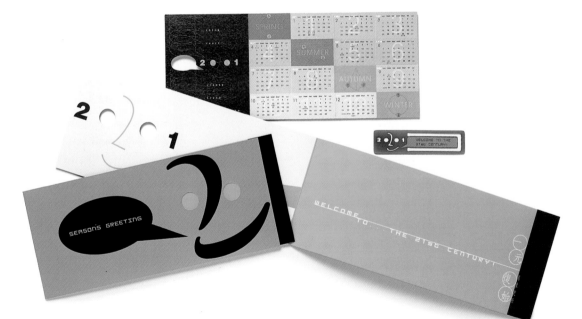

0003

0004

0005

| 0003 | Laura McFadden Design, Inc.
DESIGN: Laura McFadden Design, Inc. | 0004 | Egg Creatives
DESIGN: Jason Chen | 0005 | ARTiculation Group
DESIGN: Joseph Chan, James Ayotte |

GREETINGS **9**

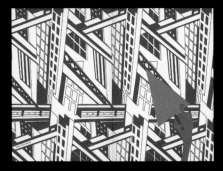

0015   Chermayeff & Geismar, Inc.
DESIGN: Steff Geissbuhler

0016

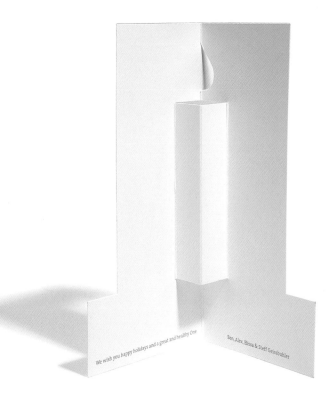

We wish you happy holidays and a great and healthy One

Ben, Alex, Elissa & Steff Geissbuhler

0017

0018

| 0016 | Sonsoles Llorens Design
DESIGN: Sonsoles Llorens | 0017 | Chermayeff & Geismar, Inc.
DESIGN: Steff Geissbuhler | 0018 | Viñas Design
DESIGN: Jaime Viñas |

12 | 1,000 GREETINGS

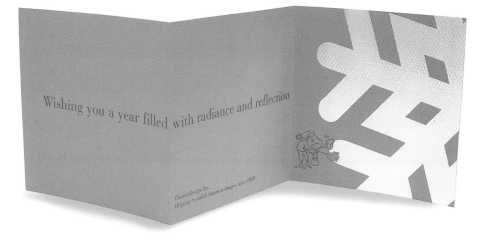

Wishing you a year filled with radiance and reflection

DanielsDesign Inc.
Helping to polish business imagery since 1969

| 0019 | Finished Art, Inc.
DESIGN: Li-Kim Goh, Marco DiCarlo, Luis Fernandez | 0020 | Daniels Design, Inc.
DESIGN: Larry Daniels |

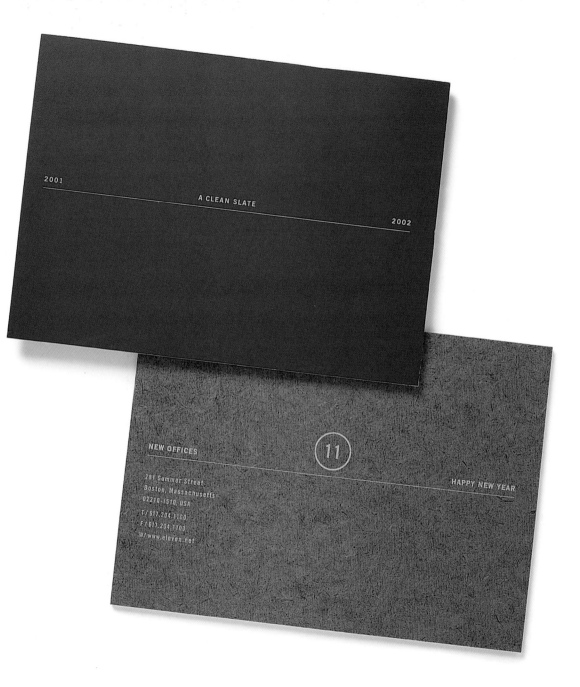

2001

A CLEAN SLATE

2002

NEW OFFICES (11) HAPPY NEW YEAR

281 Summer Street
Boston, Massachusetts
02210-1510, USA

T/ 617.204.1100
F/ 617.204.1103
W/ www.eleven.net

0021   Rick Rawlins/Work
DESIGN: Rick Rawlins

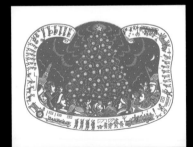

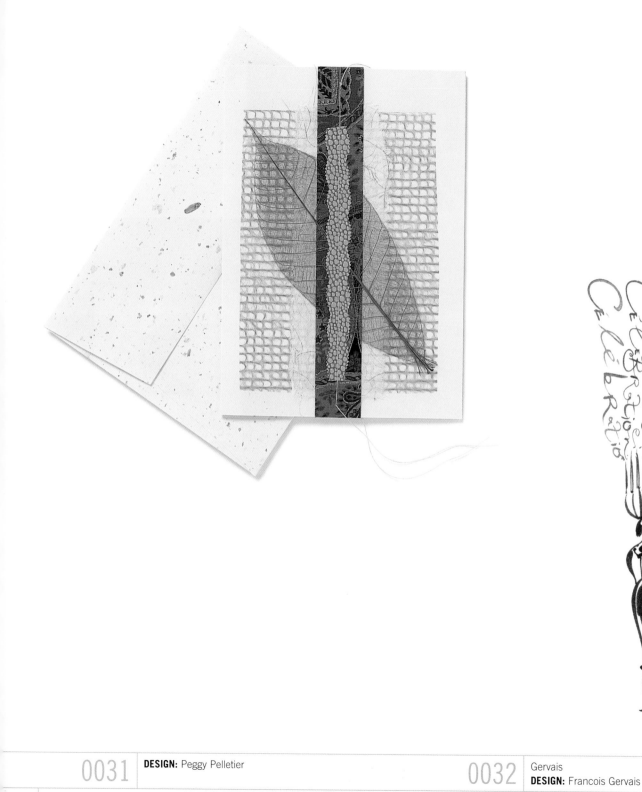

0031　**DESIGN:** Peggy Pelletier

0032　Gervais
DESIGN: Francois Gervais

0033

0034

0035

0033–0035   Muse Inspired
DESIGN: Victoria Kens

| 0036 | Shamlian Advertising
DESIGN: Jessica Paolella | 0037 | Hecht Design
DESIGN: Studio |

Tracy Design
DESIGN: Rachel Karaca, Sarah Bray

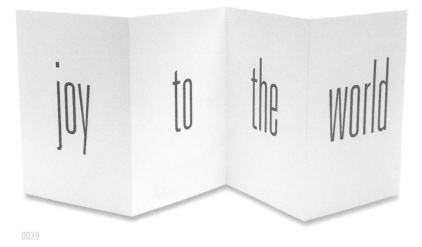

0039

0040

0041

| 0039 | Logica3 Ltd
DESIGN: Phil Oster | 0040 | **DESIGN:** Ann Conneman | 0041 | **DESIGN:** Ann Conneman |

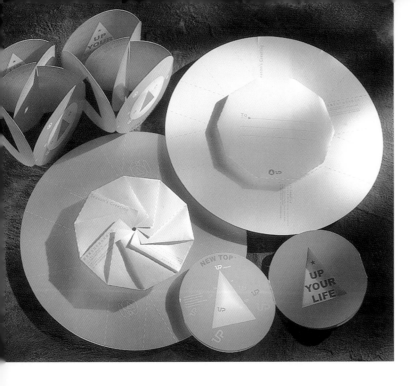

0042   UP Creative Design & Advertising
DESIGN: Jenny Pai

0043   BLACKCOFFEE
DESIGN: Mark Gallagher, Laura Savard

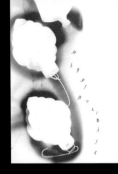

WHO
WHAT
WHERE
WHEN
WHY

May your
vowels
be airy
and light
And may
all your
consonants
be right.

l'estate

*

HAPPY
BELATED
BIRTH
DAY

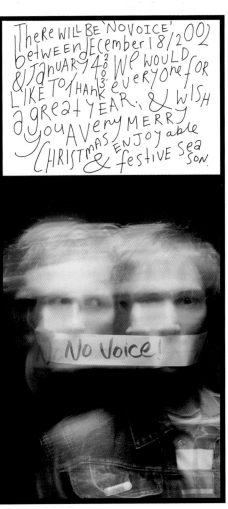

| 0053 | **DESIGN:** Swirly Designs by Lianne & Paul | 0054 | Voice
DESIGN: Scott Carslake |

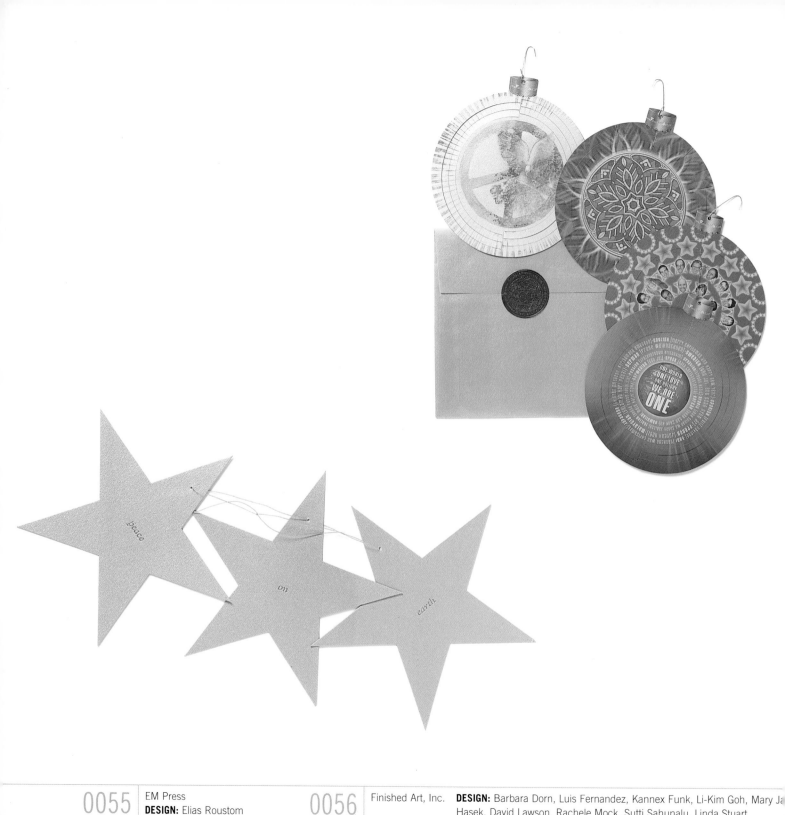

0055   EM Press
DESIGN: Elias Roustom

0056   Finished Art, Inc.   **DESIGN:** Barbara Dorn, Luis Fernandez, Kannex Funk, Li-Kim Goh, Mary Ja
Hasek, David Lawson, Rachele Mock, Sutti Sahunalu, Linda Stuart

swedish
meatballs

1 tablespoon margarine
1 onion finely diced
½ cup
1 ½ po
1 egg
½ tei
pinc
¼ t
¼

chestnut
stuffing

1 cup whole chestnuts
2 tablespoons butter
1 onion, chopped
¼ cup fresh white breadcrumbs
3 tablespoon chopped fresh parsley
3 celery sticks
freshly ground nutmeg
salt and freshly ground black pepper
1 egg, beaten

1. Make a slit in the shell of each chestnut. Place in a pan of boiling
   water and simmer for 10 minutes. Remove the outer and inner skins.
   Chop the chestnuts roughly.
2. Melt the butter in a saucepan and add the onion and chestnuts.
   Cook gently for 5 minutes.
3. Transfer to a bowl and add the breadcrumbs, parsley, celery, nutmeg
   and seasoning. Bind together with the egg.
4. Stuff turkey and roast, or place in a casserole dish and bake at 325°F
   for 30 minutes.

Serves 24

Chestnut stuffing is traditionally served with turkey at Thanksgiving or
Christmas. It's an old English recipe going back many generations and
compliments any festive meal.

0057   That's Nice LLC
       DESIGN: Erica Heitman

PAH RUN 2002 2002

MMIII

HAPPY NEW YEAR

HE KNOWS WHEN YOU ARE SLEEPING

ABSOLUTELY NO ONE,
NOT THE MAN WHO INVENTED

ABSOLUTELY NO MOM,
NOT THE ONE WHO TIED THE FIRST

MAY YOUR HOLIDAYS SPARKLE WITH JOY.

WINECOUNTRY
VINTNERS

0068

0069

0067

HAPPY HOLIDAYS
from
THE O'REILLY
FAMILY

PEACE

HAPPINESS

JOY

| 0067 | Towers Perrin
DESIGN: Media Consultants | 0068 | ARTiculation Group
DESIGN: Joseph Chan, James Ayotte | 0069 | Tom Fowler, Inc.
DESIGN: Brien O'Reilly |

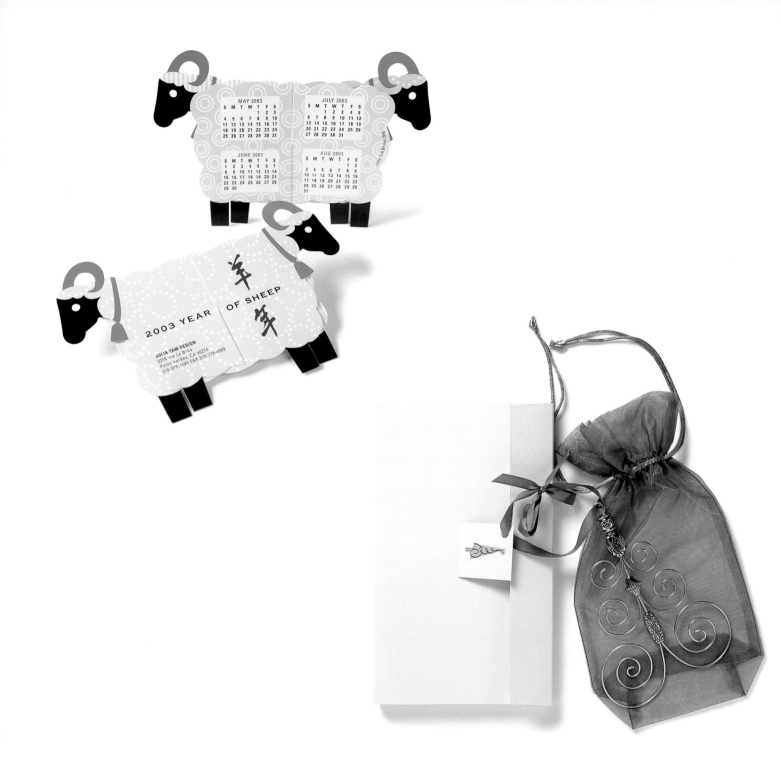

MAY 2003
S M T W T F S
          1 2 3
 4 5 6 7 8 9 10
11 12 13 14 15 16 17
18 19 20 21 22 23 24
25 26 27 28 29 30 31

JULY 2003
S M T W T F S
       1 2 3 4 5
 6 7 8 9 10 11 12
13 14 15 16 17 18 19
20 21 22 23 24 25 26
27 28 29 30 31

JUNE 2003
S M T W T F S
 1 2 3 4 5 6 7
 8 9 10 11 12 13 14
15 16 17 18 19 20 21
22 23 24 25 26 27 28
29 30

AUG 2003
S M T W T F S
                1 2
 3 4 5 6 7 8 9
10 11 12 13 14 15 16
17 18 19 20 21 22 23
24 25 26 27 28 29 30
31

2003 YEAR OF SHEEP

羊年

JULIA TAM DESIGN
2216 Via La Brea
Palos Verdes, CA 90274
310-378-2583 FAX 310-378-4589

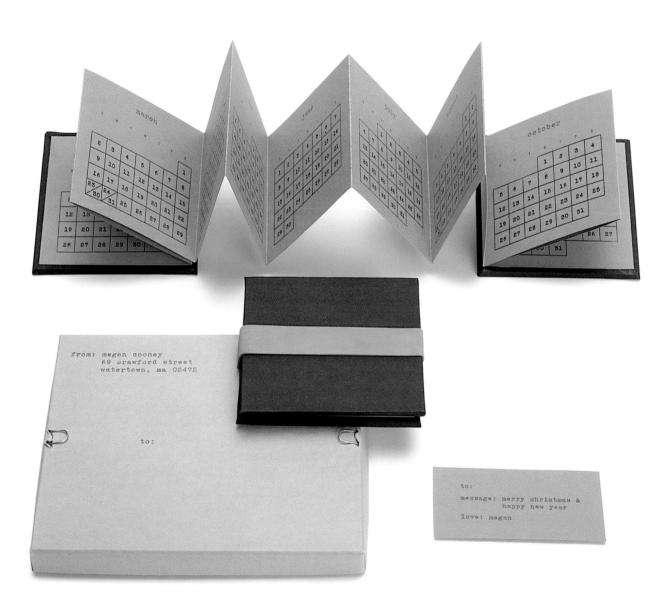

0074

0075

0073

0073   Asher Studio
DESIGN: Russ Chilcoat, Gretchen Wilis

0074   Riordan Design
DESIGN: Shirley Riordon, Amy Montgomery

0075   **DESIGN:** Michael Osborne De

30 | 1,000 GREETINGS

Valentine's Day – A Box of Love

February 2003 — We hope that this message finds you and yours in good spirits and health. We never imagined 3 years would elapse between Valentine's salutes to our family and friends, yet here we are. Please accept our most sincere apologies for the delay in production as well as our thanks to those of you who never lost faith.

While it may seem difficult to fathom, some interesting things transpired for us in the 1095 days it took to assemble our latest missive. I followed the tried and true career path from software marketing to general contracting (construction that is). As a result we have finally launched a long rumored and much awaited renovation project of our house (will most definitely be finished before the Big Dig). We are doing our part to stimulate local and international markets by single handedly carrying the local take-out industry, as the kitchen is one of the spaces undergoing renovation. In addition, anita has carried out successful capital transfusions in London, (catching the Chelsea Flower Show and the opening of the Tate Modern) and Montreal (she loves that exchange rate). Her real passion is evidenced by her inexorable quest to adorn every available inch of our yard with unique stones, twig arbors, flowering trees, climbing roses, and perennials, too numerable to mention. Even the ubiquitous gardening services so common to suburban settings blanch at the thought of maintaining our yard (have I mentioned that the butterflies love it?).

Of course, like all Americans, we were deeply disturbed by the recent events of the fall when the Anaheim Angels (that's right the Anaheim Angels) triumphed in the World Series. It is truly a strange world in which we now find ourselves. We're just happy to know you're a part of it!

Love,

anita, Andrew and coco

Our friends are shining lights.
Each of you illuminates our professional and
personal lives with joy, inspiration, humor
and a camaraderie that radiate across continents
and cultures. On December 20, we'll light
a candle in your honor. Please join us for food,
fun, and the warm glow of friendship.

Thursday, December 20, 2001, 6-8pm   4112 Swiss Ave, Dallas, Texas, 75204

Silent Night   *Holy Night*

| 0077 | David Carter Design
DESIGN: Rachel Graham | 0078 | Nassar Design
DESIGN: Margarita Encomienda, Nelida Nassar | 0079 | Hoffmann Angelic Design
DESIGN: Andrea Hoffmann |

may all your small dreams
✝ big dreams
and in-between dreams
come true this holiday season

energyenergydesign

Can I see your ID please? A blue box on your pillow
A celebrity chef is cooking dinner at your house
Hurry! It's the perfect tide, and no one's out You won 2 trips to Paris
We're naming the new constellation
after you Your Porsche Speedster convertible is ready
NASA called, and they said the ozone layer is getting smaller
Caslon has a twin sister The next number is B 5
Your non-sinking oil tanker design has been accepted
In a gap ad with Madonna And the award goes to
Where shall I put this delivery of twelve cases of Veuve
Nora Jones, table for four Take my 4 extra season passes
Move into the Cliff for a month Tiger called, 2:00 at Pasatiempo
Touchdown Guess what...you're caller number 10
Yes, we have these in size 39 and this Prada bag is 80% off
You're included in a Fortune 100 list You're offered a full scholarship
Your test is negative The Giants won the Pennant
Acme Cosmo and Cubano Sandwich And he Scores
Sotheby's called, that's a real Picasso you bought at the garage sale
Unlimited marketing budgets to reach our target

0089　energy energy design
DESIGN: Jeanette Aramburu, Stacy Buidice

0090　ZGraphics, Ltd.
DESIGN: Kris Martinez Farrell

0092

0093

0091

GUSTS

of Holiday Cheer are in your season's forecast

| 0091 | Milk Row Studio/Press
DESIGN: Keith D. Cross | 0092 | **DESIGN:** Peggy Pelletier | 0093 | **DESIGN:** Peggy Pelletier |

ICEMAN'S SON

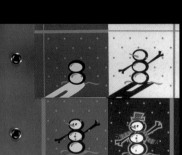

HAPPY FATHER'S DAY

0104

0103

0105

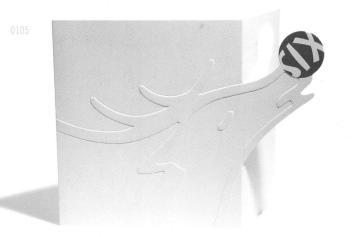

| 0103 | Sayles Graphic Design
DESIGN: John Sayles, Som Inthalangsy | 0104 | KBDA
DESIGN: Jamie Diersing | 0105 | BLANK, Inc.
DESIGN: Danielle Willis |

0106 Blue Inc.
DESIGN: Nina Max Daly

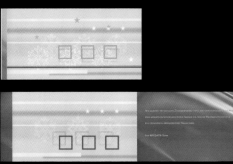

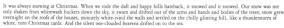

It was always snowing at Christmas. When we rode the daft and happy hills bareback, it snowed and it snowed. Our snow was not only shaken from whitewash buckets down the sky, it swam and drifted out of the arms and hands and bodies of the trees; snow grew overnight on the roofs of the houses, minutely white-ivied the walls and settled on the chilly glinting hill, like a thunderstorm of white, torn Christmas cards. And the silent one-clouded heavens drifted on to the sea.

0117

0116

0118

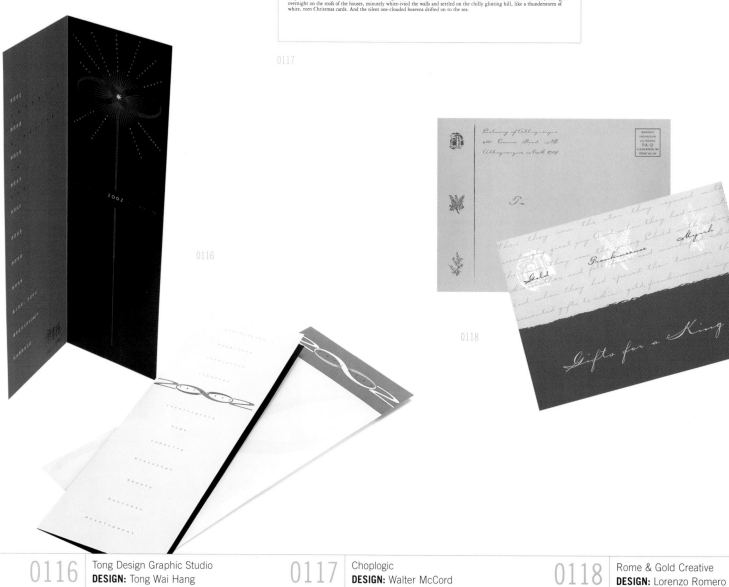

0116	Tong Design Graphic Studio	0117	Choplogic	0118	Rome & Gold Creative
	DESIGN: Tong Wai Hang		**DESIGN:** Walter McCord		**DESIGN:** Lorenzo Romero

| 0119 | UP Creative Design & Advertising Co.
DESIGN: Peter Lee | 0120 | Nassar Design
DESIGN: Margarita Encomienda, Nelida Nassar |

0131

0132

0130

thank you

HEATHER & JOE
June 8, Cape Cod

QUINN · 186 BROOKLINE ST · CAMBRIDGE, MA 02139

| 0130 | Brookline Street Design, Ltd.
DESIGN: Heather Snyder Quinn | 0131 | CC Graphic Design
DESIGN: Carolyn Crowley | 0132 | **DESIGN:** Ann Conneman |

have a **warm** and wonderful
HOLIDAY SEASON!

 SK Visual
DESIGN: Katya Lyumkis, Spencer Lum

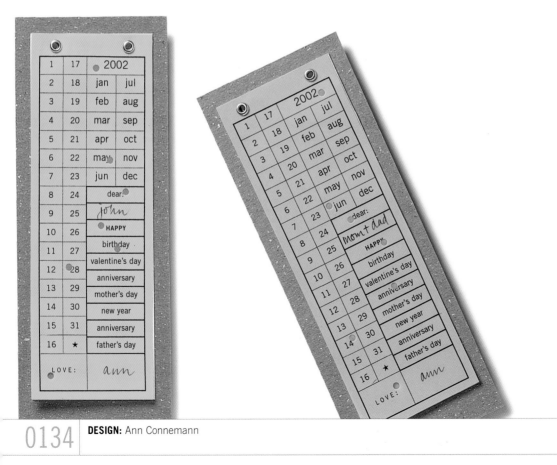

angels
may
not
come
when
you
call
them,
they
come
when
you
need
them.
Goldman

1	17	● 2002	
2	18	jan	jul
3	19	feb	aug
4	20	mar	sep
5	21	apr	oct
6	22	may	nov
7	23	jun	dec
8	24	dear:	
9	25	*john*	
10	26	● **HAPPY**	
11	27	birthday ·	
12	28	valentine's day	
13	29	anniversary	
14	30	mother's day	
15	31	new year	
16	★	anniversary	
		father's day	
L O V E :		*ann*	

2002	
1	17	jan	jul
2	18	feb	aug
3	19	mar	sep
4	20	apr	oct
5	21	may	nov
6	22	jun	dec
7	23	dear:	
8	24	*mom+dad*	
9	25	**HAPPY**	
10	26	birthday	
11	27	valentine's day	
12	28	anniversary	
13	29	mother's day	
14	30	new year	
15	31	anniversary	
16	★	father's day	
L O V E :		*ann*	

0134   **DESIGN:** Ann Connemann

0135   hagopian ink
DESIGN: Christina Hagopian

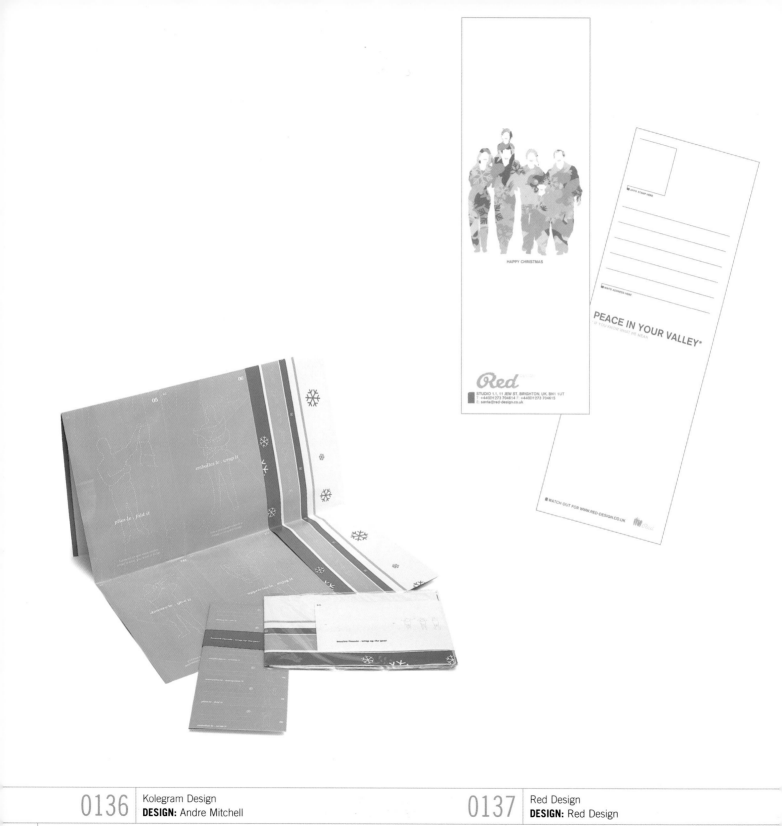

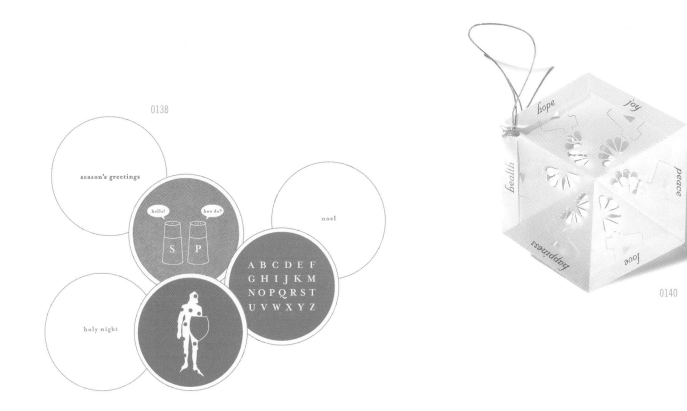

0139

0138

0140

| 0138 | Megan Webber Design
DESIGN: Megan Webber, Wendy Carnegie | 0139 | Sudduth Design Co.
DESIGN: Toby Sudduth | 0140 | Brauer Design Inc.
DESIGN: Bruce Erik Brauer |

GREETINGS **47**

0141   Design Dairy
DESIGN: H. Locascio

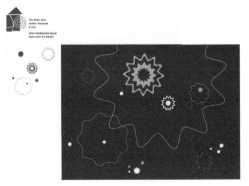

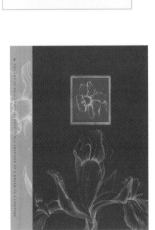

A loving hug
A kiss or two
A ton of friends (and family too)
A hint of laughter
A dash of fun
A splash of good cheer...

Happy Holidays
from Splash Interactive

Recipe for Holiday Spirits

0151   Splash Interactive
DESIGN: Ivy Wong

0152   After Hours Creative
DESIGN: After Hours Creative

0153 Metzler & Associes
DESIGN: A. Pavion

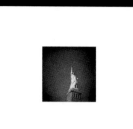

IN THIS
SEASON
OF HOLIDAY JOY
WE WISH
TO EXTEND TO YOU
OUR BEST WISHES
FOR THE
NEW YEAR

PEACE, JOY & FRIENDSHIP
FROM YOUR FRIENDS AT FIREBELLY DESIGN

0165   Firebelly Design
DESIGN: Mikel Rosenthal

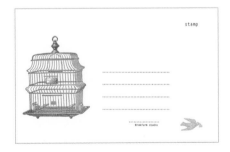

0166	Indian Hill Press	0169	**DESIGN:** Sayre Gaydos	0172	**DESIGN:** Sayre Gaydos
	DESIGN: Daniel A. Waters	0170	W. C. Burgard Illustration	0173	Smudge Ink
0167	Indian Hill Press		**DESIGN:** W. C. Burgard		**DESIGN:** Kate Saliba
	DESIGN: Daniel A. Waters	0171	**DESIGN:** Sayre Gaydos	0174	**DESIGN:** Sayre Gaydos
0168	Indian Hill Press				
	DESIGN: Daniel A. Waters				

0175

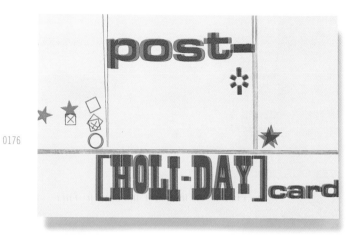

0176

0177

| 0175 | graphische formgebung **DESIGN:** Herbert Rohsiepe | 0176 | **DESIGN:** Jennifer Eaton Alden | 0177 | Wilson Harvey **DESIGN:** Wai Lau |

0178	Rick Johnson & Company **DESIGN:** Tim McGrath	
0179	Riordon Design **DESIGN:** Amy Montgomery	

CARDS TO SEND *To friends*

WE ALL SHOULD WRITE
MORE OFTEN THAN WE DO
A FEW SIMPLE WORDS THAT
ARE HONEST AND TRUE.

TO FRIENDS WHO HAVE ADDED
SO MUCH TO OUR DAYS
AND HAVE SOMEHOW SURVIVED
OUR SELF-ABSORBED WAYS.

JUST A LINE ON A CARD
TO SAY SOMETHING SMALL,
BECAUSE LIFE IS TOO SHORT
TO SAY NOTHING AT ALL.

0180 **ARTiculation Group**
DESIGN: Joseph Chan, Wilson Lam, Helen Ng, Karin Fukuzawa

THERE IS NO JOY

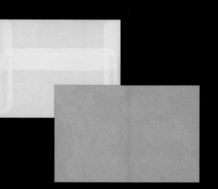

ALEX, I'LL TAKE
LOVE
FOR A HUNDRED

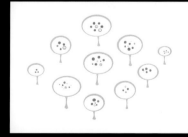

0190   That's Nice, LLC
DESIGN: Phil Evans

0191   Whitenoise
DESIGN: Juue Turkington

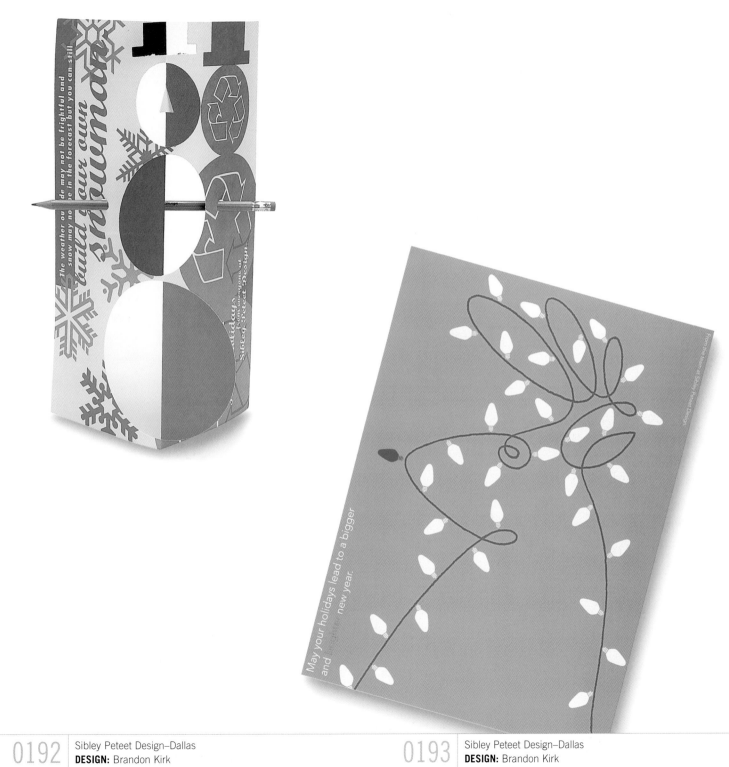

The weather outside may not be frightful and snow may not be in the forecast but you can still build your own snowman.

Happy Holidays from everyone at Sibley Peteet Design.

May your holidays lead to a bigger and brighter new year.

From the team at Sibley Peteet Design

0192 Sibley Peteet Design–Dallas
DESIGN: Brandon Kirk

0193 Sibley Peteet Design–Dallas
DESIGN: Brandon Kirk

0195

0196

0194

| 0194 | KO création
DESIGN: Pol Baril, Annie Lachapelle | 0195 | **DESIGN:** Sayre Gaydos | 0196 | Get Smart Design Company
DESIGN: GSDC Staff |

0206   **DESIGN:** Form Funf Bremen

0207   Gervais/Citron Vert
DESIGN: Francois Gervais

McCullough

Our entire staff
wishes you
a very Merry Christmas.

0209   McCullough Creative Group, Inc.
DESIGN: McCullough Creative Team

0210   **DESIGN:** Sayre Gaydos

I LIKE

I WANNA KISS

I WANT

I MISS

I LOVE

I'M HOT FOR

I ADORE

I WAS JUST THINKING ABOUT

YOU

I just do. If we were in school I'd pull your hair. If we were kitties, I'd bite your neck. Who cares what Freud would say about it-I think there's something for us here. You in?

TO:

FROM

DAIRY
WHEELIES©2003
www.designdairy.com

ANNIVERSARY

NEW BABY

HOLIDAYS

VALENTINE'S DAY

TRAILS

HOUSEWARMING

NEW YEAR

BIRTHDAY

HAPPY

You make a fine contribution to the institution. You are heroes of coupling, of compromise, of mutual respect. Cheers and many, many more.

TO:

FROM

DAIRY
WHEELIES©2003
www.designdairy.com

0220   **DESIGN:** Dairy

0221   **DESIGN:** Dairy

Peace, health and love
we wish to you
for all the holidays
and two thousand two

Elissa & Steff
Alex & Ben
Geissbuhler

0223

0222

0224

Hang a SHINING STAR
Upon the highest bough...

2002

0222 Egg Creatives
DESIGN: Kevin Lee

0223 Chermayeff & Geismar, Inc.
DESIGN: Steff Geissbuhler

0224 Transcend
DESIGN: Hung Q. Tran

GREETINGS **69**

0225   energy energy design
DESIGN: Jeanette Aramburu

But we're hopeful. It's a brand new year, a new TV season and soon we'll all be zipping around on those crazy Segway™ Human Transporters. In any case, next year is sure to bring more great opportunities for us to not only push the creative envelope, but even lick it.

happy holidays | kendall ross

Here's the deal. We sat around for hours trying to come up with a few pithy, witty concepts for the annual holiday card. Let's face it. The economy is in the toilet, Britney broke up with Justin and "The Bachelor" picked the one we didn't like.

kendall ross
brand development design
1904 Third Avenue, Suite 1005 Seattle, Washington 98101 USA
+1 206 262.0540   +1 206 262.0693   www.kendallross.com

0227

HOLIDAY CHARACTERS

0226

A snowflake fell into my hand,
a tiny, fragile gem,
a frosty crystal flowerlet
with petals, but no stem.

A Snowflake Fell

0228

0226 Rickabaugh Graphics
DESIGN: Eric Rickabaugh

0227 Kendall Ross
DESIGN: Scott Fricsen, Helen Kong

0228 Visual Solutions
DESIGN: Cynthia Anderson

GREETINGS | **71**

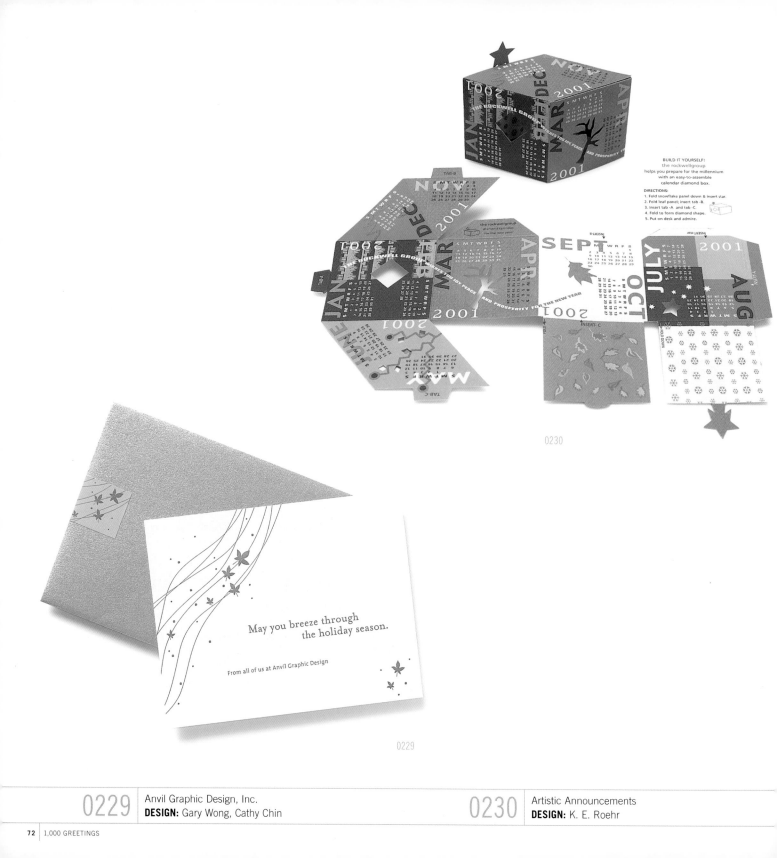

BUILD IT YOURSELF!
the rockwellgroup
helps you prepare for the millennium
with an easy-to-assemble
calendar diamond box.

DIRECTIONS:
1. Fold snowflake panel down & insert star.
2. Fold leaf panel; insert tab -B.
3. Insert tab -A and tab -C.
4. Fold to form diamond shape.
5. Put on desk and admire.

May you breeze through
the holiday season.

From all of us at Anvil Graphic Design

0229

0230

0229   Anvil Graphic Design, Inc.
DESIGN: Gary Wong, Cathy Chin

0230   Artistic Announcements
DESIGN: K. E. Roehr

0232

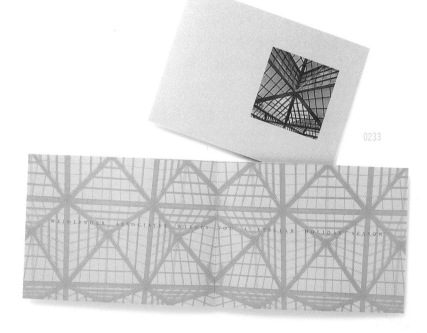

0233

0231

| 0231 | Gervais
DESIGN: Francois Gervais | 0232 | Mindwalk Design Group, Inc.
DESIGN: Michael Huggins | 0233 | Nassar Design
DESIGN: Margarita Encomienda, Nelida Nassar |

SUGAR
AND SPICE
AND ALL THAT'S
NICE

SLUGS
AND SNAILS
AND PUPPY DOGS'
TAILS

BON VOYAGE

AND
MANY
MORE

21
AGAIN

WHOOPS
A
DAISY

COOCHY
COOCHY
COO!

GET
WELL
AT ONCE

OLD
NEW
BORROWED
BLUE

0244

America Online commissioned noted artist Seymour Chwast to create this exclusive holiday illustration. For us, it symbolizes how AOL and its partners collaborate to connect America to information, entertainment and ideas.

As a celebration of what we have accomplished together, enclosed you will find a one-of-a-kind piece of the "puzzle," as a reminder that you are a unique and vital member of this highly valued partnership.

Peace.

0243

0245

| 0243 | And Partners
DESIGN: David Schimmel | 0244 | Sonsoles Llorens Design
DESIGN: Sonsoles Llorens | 0245 | **DESIGN:** Dairy |

GREETINGS **75**

Nassar Design
DESIGN: Margarita Encomienda, Nelida Nassar

Winter
Peppermints

SPRING
Jellybean

SUMMER
Sunflower Seeds

FALL
Chocolate
Covered Peanuts

Wishing You Seasons of Joy
Happy New Year

He wore blue suede shoes, shook his pelvis,

and was known by the other elves as Elf-vis

Merry Mix-Mess

| 0247 | Studio J
DESIGN: Angela Jackson | 0248 | McCullough Creative Group, Inc.
DESIGN: Greg Dietzenbach |

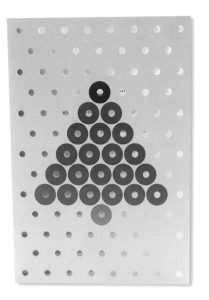

0250

0251

0249

0249   Brookline Street Design, Ltd.
DESIGN: Heather Snyder Quinn

0250   IC Company In-house
DESIGN: Vibeke Nodskov

0251   BLACKCOFFEE
DESIGN: Mark Gallagher, Laura Savard

78   1,000 GREETINGS

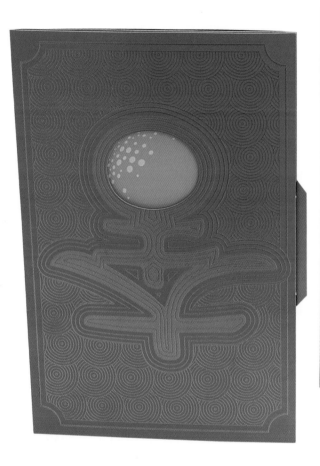

0252 | Egg Creatives
DESIGN: Lim Choon Pin

falling leaves

summer nights

spring blossoms

HAPPY**MAY**DAY!

SINCE ANCIENT TIMES, MAY FIRST HAS BEEN A DAY FOR OUTDOOR FESTIVALS. THE ENGLISH HAVE OBSERVED MAY DAY SINCE MEDIEVAL TIMES. PEOPLE WOULD GO INTO THE FOREST TO GATHER FLOWERS AND BRANCHES OF TREES TO DECORATE THEIR HOMES. A MAY QUEEN WAS CROWNED TO REIGN OVER THE GAMES AND DANCING AROUND A STREAMER-LADEN MAY POLE. *But streamer-laden poles aside, what's the happs?*

Take the first right, then next left just after the roundabout, carry on, it should be coming up on your left. That's it. Almost there. Now go straight up to the top. Take the small opening and go all the way down. Stand up and go through to the next room. Find stocking.

Season's Greetings

DESIGN: Smudge Ink   0256   **DESIGN:** Smudge Ink   0259   **DESIGN:** Smudge Ink

DESIGN: Dairy   0257   Indian Hill Press   0260   Roundel

DESIGN: Sayre Gaydos   **DESIGN:** Daniel A. Waters   **DESIGN:** Paul Ingle

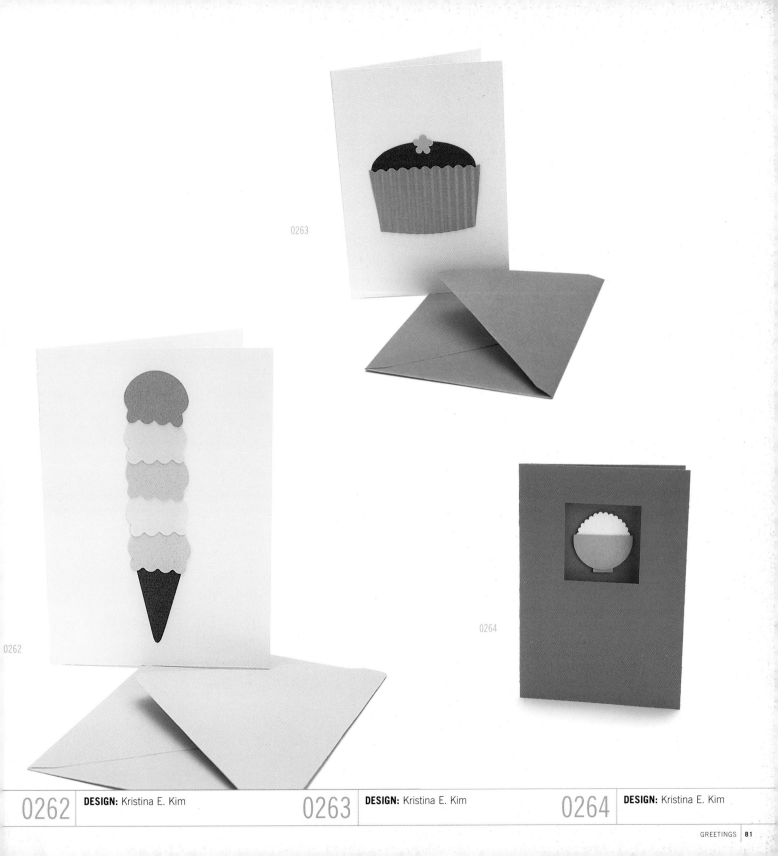

| 0262 | **DESIGN:** Kristina E. Kim | 0263 | **DESIGN:** Kristina E. Kim | 0264 | **DESIGN:** Kristina E. Kim |

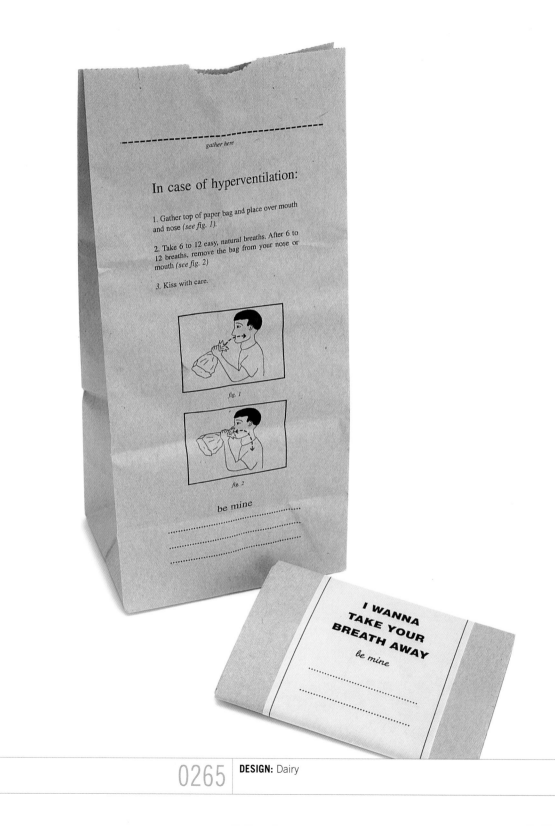

In case of hyperventilation:

1. Gather top of paper bag and place over mouth and nose *(see fig. 1)*.

2. Take 6 to 12 easy, natural breaths. After 6 to 12 breaths, remove the bag from your nose or mouth *(see fig. 2)*

3. Kiss with care.

fig. 1

fig. 2

be mine

I WANNA
TAKE YOUR
BREATH AWAY
be mine

0265 **DESIGN:** Dairy

 0266 Miro Design
DESIGN: Judy Glenzer

 0267 Swirly Designs by Lianne & Paul
DESIGN: Paul Stoddard

Thank you for the beautiful _____.
Not only will it make an excellent addition
to our _____, but it makes us
_____ every time we look at it. You
were so _____ to think of us.

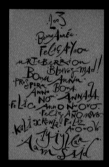

I love you more than_____:

❑ mashed potatoes
❑ sleep
❑ champagne
❑ all of the above

0277 | Michael Osborne Design
DESIGN: Paul Kagiwada, Michelle Regen Bogen

0278

0280

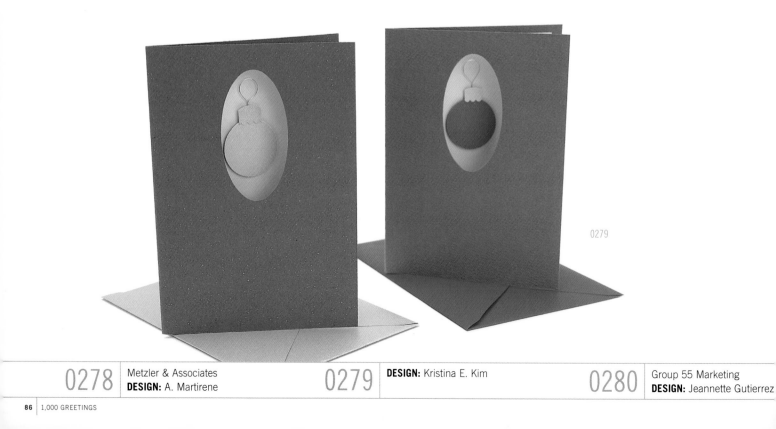

0279

| 0278 | Metzler & Associates
DESIGN: A. Martirene | 0279 | **DESIGN:** Kristina E. Kim | 0280 | Group 55 Marketing
DESIGN: Jeannette Gutierrez |

I was just thinking about_____:

❑ the stock market

❑ current events

❑ the meaning of life

❑ you

I miss _____:

❑ the eighties

❑ puberty

❑ beta

❑ you

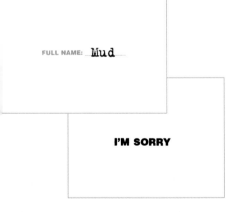

FULL NAME: Mud

I'M SORRY

HAPPYFLAG DAY!

FLAG DAY, THE ANNIVERSARY OF THE FLAG RESOLUTION OF 1777, WAS OFFICIALLY ESTABLISHED BY PRESIDENT WILSON ON MAY 30TH, 1916. IT WASN'T UNTIL 1949, THAT PRESIDENT TRUMAN SIGNED AN ACT OF CONGRESS DESIGNATING JUNE 14TH OF EACH YEAR AS NATIONAL FLAG DAY. *That said, how's it hanging?*

0281   Smudge Ink
     DESIGN: Kate Saliba

0282   Gervais
     DESIGN: Francois Gervais

0283   **DESIGN:** Dairy

0284   **DESIGN:** Dairy

0285   Gervais
     DESIGN: Francois Gervais

0286   **DESIGN:** Kristina E. Kim

0287   **DESIGN:** Dairy

0288   Wallace Church
     DESIGN: Stan Church

0289   **DESIGN:** Dairy

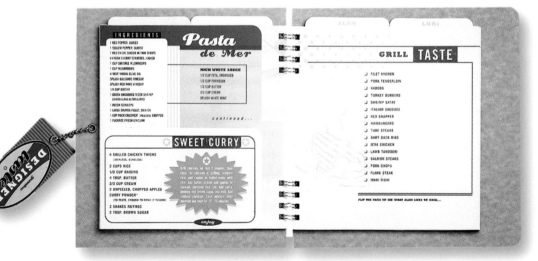

0290 Riordon Design
DESIGN: Amy Montgomery, Sharon Pece

The odds are good that it will be a Happy New Year. Greetings from Paul Shaw/Letter Design and Peter Kruty Editions.

HAPPY

HUMBLE

HOLIDAYS

TO YOU

FROM US

HUMBLE JOURNEY
F I L M S

ERIQ LA SALLE   BUTCH ROBINSON   CAMILLE TUCKER
ALLISON DAVIS   YOLIE MARTINEZ

SO YOUR ODOMETER
JUST CLICKED OVER THE OTHER DAY

SOME QUESTIONS
THAT HAVE NOT ONCE BEEN UTTERED:

IN ONE HOUR
I CAN MAKE 20 3-MINUTE EGGS

FOR ONE DAY
INSIST THAT EVERYONE GREET YOU

OPPORTUNITY
IS NOT JUST KNOCKING

IF YOU HAD KETCHUP
PACKETS IN YOUR GLOVE BOX

WHY? WHY? WHY?
WHY IS THE SKY BLUE? WHY DOES

DON'T GET YOUR MEAT
WHERE YOU GET YOUR BREAD

THE DAY YOU
SAID YES WAS NOT

Best Wishes for 2003
from
EM Press

Elias, Maggie, & Rose

Illustration based on weathervane design by George Washington.
Grant Will Press, New Bedford, Mass.

0302

0304

dancing **bright** *shining*

memories *ornaments* *and joy*

from holidays **for the** *past* *future*

warm wishes

Kehoe + Kehoe Design Associates Inc.

Deborah Kehoe

Michael Bemis

Jeffrey Forland

Kevin Horn

0303

| 0302 | EM Press
DESIGN: Elias Roustom | 0303 | Kehoe & Kehoe Design Associates
DESIGN: Deborah Kehoe | 0304 | UP Creative Design & Advertising Co.
DESIGN: Javen LIn |

GREETINGS **91**

0305 Hutchinson Associates, Inc.
DESIGN: Jerry Hutchinson

| 0306 | John Kneapler Design
DESIGN: Holly Buckley, John Kneapler | 0307 | hagopian ink
DESIGN: Christina Hagopian |

0309

0308

0310

| 0308 | Mirage Design
DESIGN: Lynette Allaire | 0309 | Nassar Design
DESIGN: Margarita Encomienda, Nelida Nassar | 0310 | Design Dairy
DESIGN: H. Locascio |

0311–0313   **DESIGN:** Kristina E. Kim

Hope your holidays are filled with the anticipation of children – the sound of church bells on a starlit night – presents that rattle when shaken – extra Scotch tape – the crisp scent of evergreen – magical memories – homemade peanut brittle – laughter and love.

0314   And Partners
DESIGN: David Schimmel

0315   W. C. Burgard Illustration
DESIGN: W. C. Burgard

WHITE OUT?

WHITE RHINO PRODUCTIONS INC.
41 SECOND AVE.
BURLINGTON, MA 01803

WHITE RHINO!

HAPPY HOLIDAYS FROM YOUR FRIENDS AT
WHITE RHINO PRODUCTIONS INC.

0327

Never knock on Death's
door; ring the bell and
run away! Death really
hates that!
—Matt Frewer
as Dr. Mike Stratford
in Doctor, Doctor

0326

Happy Holidays from Steve Fleshman

Ring out the Old
Ring in the New

www.dr-2.com

| 0325 | graphische formgebung
DESIGN: Herbert Rohsiepe | 0326 | DR2
DESIGN: Steven D. Fleshman | 0327 | White Rhino
DESIGN: Athena Hermann |

| 0328 | Mirage Design
DESIGN: Lynette Allaire | 0329 | Refinery Design Company
DESIGN: Julie Schmalz | 0330 | Design Dairy
DESIGN: H. Locascio |

winter wonderland

M M
O

HAPPY MOTHER'S DAY

IF YOU LEAVE ME

can i come too?

baby

FOR MY
BETTER
1/2

smile

AND BABY
MAKES
THREE

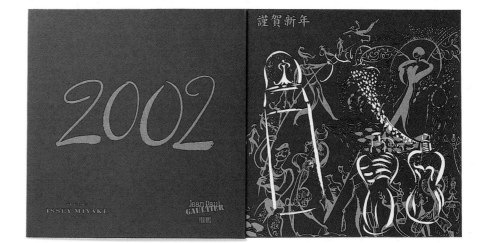

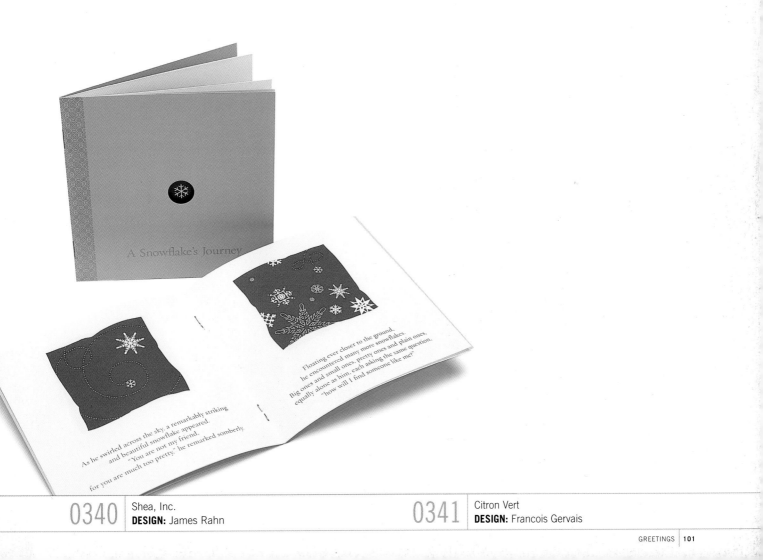

| 0340 | Shea, Inc.
DESIGN: James Rahn | 0341 | Citron Vert
DESIGN: Francois Gervais |

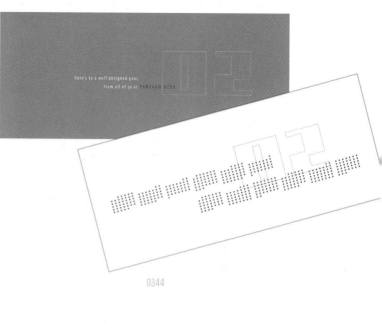

0344

0342

0343

| 0342 | Emery Vincent Design
DESIGN: Emery Vincent Design | 0343 | **DESIGN:** Vrontikis Design Office | 0344 | Pangaro Beer
DESIGN: David Salafia, Joanna DeFazio |

emma

0354

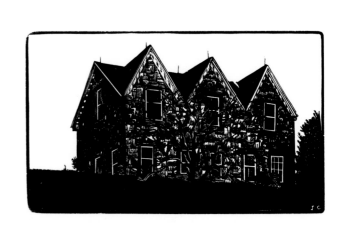

0356

0355

| 0354 | **DESIGN:** John Cameron | 0355 | **DESIGN:** John Cameron | 0356 | **DESIGN:** John Cameron |

CELEBRATE

your family

| 0357 | IE Design
DESIGN: Marcie Carson, Richard Haynie | 0358 | After Hours Creative
DESIGN: After Hours Creative |

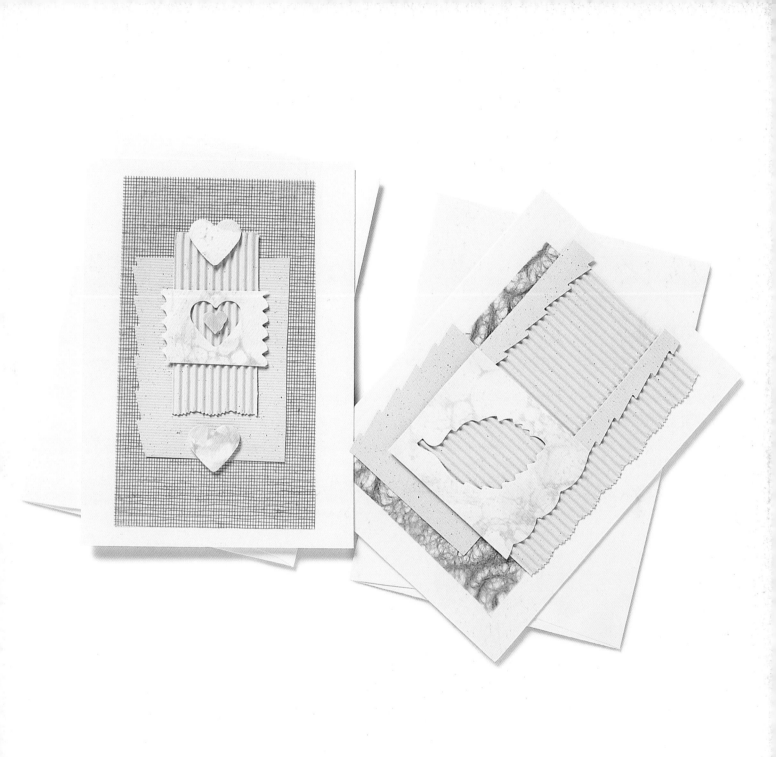

0368   **DESIGN:** Peggy Pelletier

0369   **DESIGN:** Peggy Pelletier

0372

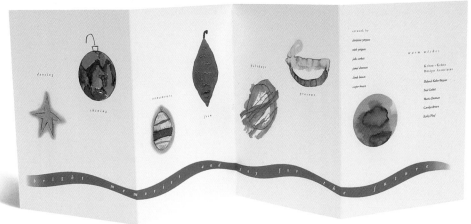

0371

| 0370 | Egg Creatives
DESIGN: Jason Chen | 0371 | Kehoe & Kehoe Design Associates
DESIGN: Deborah Kehoe | 0372 | d/g brussels
DESIGN: Sally Orr |

108 | 1,000 GREETINGS

0382—0386   Fiddlesticks Press
DESIGN: Lynne Amft

re·solve (r-zlv) v. re-solved, re-solv-ing, re-solves v. tr. 1. To make a firm decision about. 2. To cause (a person) to reach a decision. 3. To decide or express by formal vote. 4. To change or convert: My resentment resolved itself into resignation. 5. To find a solution to; solve. See Synonyms at solve. 6. To remove or dispel (doubts). 7. To bring to a usually successful conclusion: resolve a conflict. 8. Medicine. To cause reduction of (an inflammation, for example). 9. Music. To cause (a tone or chord) to progress from dissonance to consonance. 10. Chemistry. To separate (an optically inactive compound or mixture) into its optically active constituents. 11. To render parts of (an image) visible and distinct. 12. Mathematics. To separate (a vector, for example) into coordinate components. 13. To melt or dissolve (something). 14. Archaic. To separate (something) into constituent parts. HOPING YOUR NEW YEAR IS HAPPY, RESOLUTE, AND THAT EVERYTHING IS WHERE IT'S SUPPOSED TO BE. With love from JACKIE & MIRO.

re·solve (r-zlv) v. re-solved, re-solv-ing, re-solves reach a decision. 3. To decide or express by formal vote. 4. To tion. 5. To find a solution to; solve. See Synonyms at solve. 6. T conclusion: resolve a conflict. 8. Medicine. To cause reduction chord) to progress from dissonance to consonance. 10. Chemist its optically active constituents. 11. To render parts of (an image) example) into coordinate components. 13. To melt or disse constituent parts. HOPING YOUR NEW YEAR IS HAPPY SUPPOSED TO BE. With love from Jackie & Michael

HAPPY**ARBOR**DAY!

ARBOR DAY IS A NATIONALLY CELEBRATED OBSERVANCE THAT ENCOURAGES TREE PLANTING AND TREE CARE. FOUNDED BY J. STERLING MORTON IN NEBRASKA IN 1872, NATIONAL ARBOR DAY IS CELEBRATED EACH YEAR ON THE LAST FRIDAY IN APRIL, SO YES, HAPPY ARBOR DAY, *but really I just wanted to say hiya.*

0390

HAPPY**BOXING**DAY!

THE DAY AFTER CHRISTMAS, THE FEAST OF ST. STEPHEN IS BETTER KNOWN AS BOXING DAY. THE TERM MAY COME FROM THE OPENING OF CHURCH POOR BOXES THAT DAY; OR MAYBE FROM THE BOXES WITH WHICH APPRENTICES COLLE[CTED] MONEY AT THE DOORS OF THEIR MASTERS' CLIENTS, e[...] *way, i was just wondering how you were[...]*

0389

HAPPY**GROUNDHOG**DAY!

FEBRUARY 2 IS GROUNDHOG DAY, THE DAY THAT THE GROUNDHOG COMES OUT OF HIS HOLE AFTER WINTER HIBERNATION TO LOOK FOR HIS SHADOW. BY SEEING IT, HE FORETELLS SIX MORE WEEKS OF BAD WHETHER AND GOES BACK INTO HIS HOLE. IF HE DOESN'T, HE STAYS OUT. INDICATING THAT SPRING IS NEAR. STATISTICAL EVIDENCE DOES NOT SUPPORT THIS TRADITION, *but I thought it a really fine reason to write and say i was thinking about you.*

0391

| 0389 | **DESIGN:** Dairy | 0390 | **DESIGN:** Dairy | 0391 | **DESIGN:** Dairy |

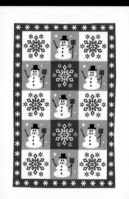

IT'S NOT THAT I'M
OBSESSED WITH YOU

Peace on Earth

Happy New Yea

mARTin lemelMAN · www.martart.com · 1286 Country Club Road Allentown, PA 18106 · 1(888) 412-1960

CAPE COD

It the bared and bended arm of Massachusetts
the shoulder is at Buzzard's Bay,
the elbow or crazy-bone at Cape Mallebarre,
the wrist at Truro,
and the sandy fist at Provincetown.

❖ Thoreau

cape cod

CAPE COD

CAPE COD

CAPE COD

FALMOUTH SANDWICH BOURNE MASHPEE
BARNSTABLE HYANNIS YARMOUTH DENNIS
BREWSTER HARWICH CHATHAM ORLEANS
EASTHAM WELLFLEET TRURO PROVINCETOWN
NANTUCKET AND MARTHA'S VINEYARD

0401—0405 | hagopian ink
DESIGN: Christina Hagopian

light, seeking light doth light of light beguile....
William Shakespeare (1564–1616)

Peace
The Stubbins Associates Inc.

0406 John Kneapler Design
DESIGN: Colleen Shea

0407 Nassar Design
DESIGN: Margarita Encomienda, Nelida Nassar

ETHAN MCGREGOR RAWLINS
9 21 02

ANNOUNCEMENTS

CREATED with

LOVE

CARRIED with

HOPE and

WELCOMED with

JOY

Elizabeth Grace

JAKUBEK CRAWFORD

daughter of
ALAN JAKUBEK and CAROLINE CRAWFORD
was welcomed into the world
at 11:08 am on Tuesday, March 25th, 2003

7 pounds, 8 ounces
20 inches long

"A baby is God's opinion that life should go on."
Carl Sandburg

0409

Alexander Ku
and Jane Yeomans Ku
are happy to announce the arrival of:
LEO XAVIER MING-RYH KU
— Born February 1st 2002 —
New York City

0408

JACKSON

SEAN & LISA WEBBER
Proudly Announce
the birth of their son

JACK SON

0410

| 0408 | Peter Kruty Editions
DESIGN: Alexander Ku | 0409 | Kehoe & Kehoe Design Associates
DESIGN: Deborah Kehoe | 0410 | Webber Design Werks
DESIGN: Sean Webber |

0411   **DESIGN:** Red Design

0412   angryporcupine_design
DESIGN: Cheryl Roder-Quill

0422   plus design, inc.
DESIGN: Anita Meyer, Karin Fickett, Dina Zaccagnini, Matthew Monk, Jan Baker

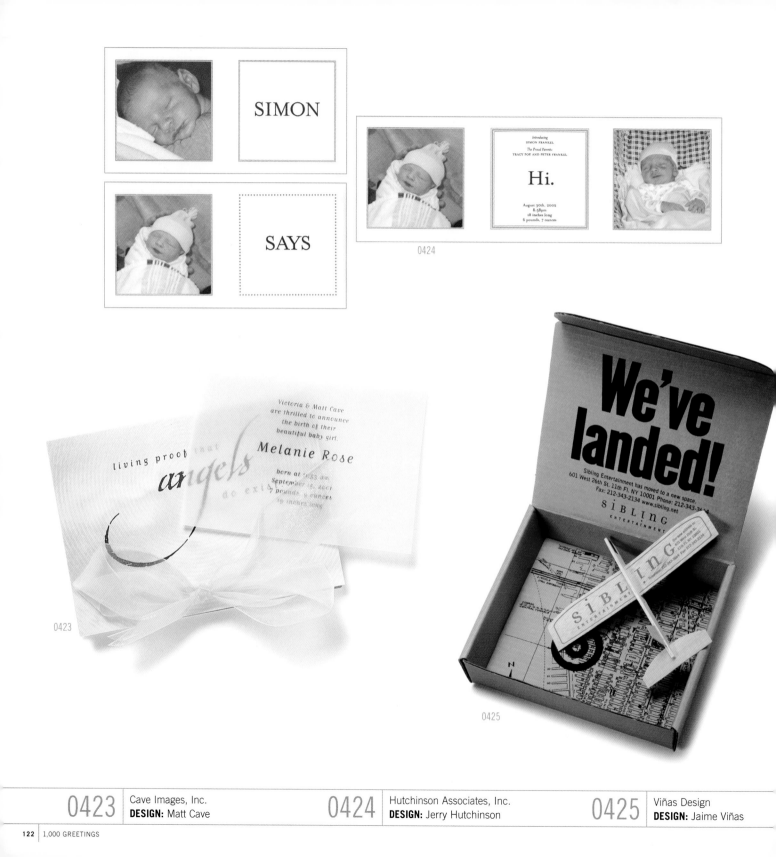

SIMON

SAYS

Introducing
SIMON FRANKEL
The Proud Parents:
TRACY POE AND PETER FRANKEL

Hi.

August 30th, 2002
8:58pm
18 inches long
6 pounds, 7 ounces

0424

Victoria & Matt Cave
are thrilled to announce
the birth of their
beautiful baby girl.

Melanie Rose

born at 11:55 a.m.
September 18, 2001
7 pounds, 9 ounces
19 inches long

living proof that
angels
do exist

0423

We've landed!

Sibling Entertainment has moved to a new space.
601 West 26th St. 11th Fl. NY 10001 Phone: 212-343-3614
Fax: 212-343-2134 www.sibling.net

SIBLING
ENTERTAINMENT

0425

| 0423 | Cave Images, Inc. **DESIGN:** Matt Cave | 0424 | Hutchinson Associates, Inc. **DESIGN:** Jerry Hutchinson | 0425 | Viñas Design **DESIGN:** Jaime Viñas |

Marco Beretta

21 de noviembre de 2002 - 1.35 am - 3,120 kg - 48,5 cm

0426

0428

10 YEARS OF GRAPHIC DESIGN, OUT THE WINDOW...

We've moved (2 doors down from our old office). The hard part is over, but we could still use your help...
On April 1, 2003, between 11am and 2 pm, come and celebrate our 10th anniversary with us.
Drop by our new studio and join us for an open house and a free lunch.
Please call 327-9894 by March 28 to RSVP.

...AND DOWN THE STREET...

andersonthomas◎

0427

| 0426 | España Design **DESIGN:** Cecilia España | 0427 | Anderson Thomas Design **DESIGN:** Kristi Smith | 0428 | Porto & Martinez Design Studio **DESIGN:** Bruno Porto |

ANNOUNCEMENTS **123**

| 0429 | Rule 29
DESIGN: Justin Ahrens | 0430 | Tom Fowler, Inc.
DESIGN: Brien O'Reilly |

ETHAN McGREGOR RAWLINS
9 21 02

0431 Rick Rawlins/Work
DESIGN: Rick Rawlins

0442

0441

My baby
sister...

0443

| 0441 | Burgard Design
DESIGN: Todd Burgard | 0442 | Wilson Harvey
DESIGN: Ben Wood | 0443 | Viñas Design
DESIGN: Jaime Viñas |

0444   Design 5
DESIGN: Ron Nikkel

0445   Cave Images, Inc.
DESIGN: Matt Cave

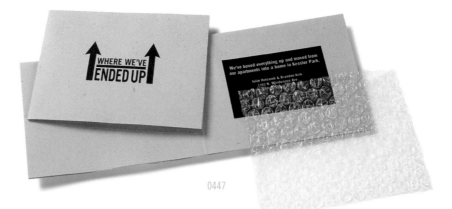

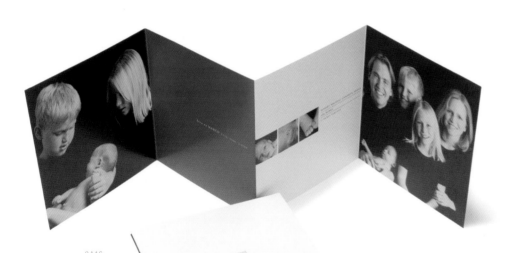

0446
Noon
DESIGN: Cinthia Wen

0447
Sibley Peteet Design—Dallas
DESIGN: Brandon Kirk

0448
Alterpop
DESIGN: Christopher Simmons

ANNOUNCEMENTS **129**

0449   Cave Images
DESIGN: David Edmundson

mackerel sky Architecture

Curious. Unusual. Motivated.
5715 Chilham Road
Baltimore, MD 21209
phone 410.664.1960
fax 410.664.1960
email mhaines@mackerelskyarchitecture.com
www.mackerelskyarchitecture.com

We've flown north

mackerel sky
moved
to a new location

0451

HN Media & Marketing
275 Madison Avenue, 22nd Floor
New York, New York 10016

0450

SAME OLD* CHEESE.

BRAND NEW OFFICES.

PARMIGIANO REGGIANO
CONSORZIO DEL FORMAGGIO
U.S. INFORMATION OFFICE

Nancy Radke *Director*
CCP-Certified Culinary Professional
nradke@parmigiano-reggiano.com

404 Oak Street, Suite 25
Syracuse NY 13203-2997
315.475.0475

Martha Williams *Cheese Girl*
mwilliams@parmigiano-reggiano.com

FAX.475.0557

0452

| 0450 | And Partners
DESIGN: David Schimmel, Sarah Hollowood | 0451 | BLANK, Inc.
DESIGN: Danielle Willis | 0452 | Marty Blake Graphic Design
DESIGN: Marty Blake |

0453   Selbert Perkins Design
DESIGN: Avvi Raquel-Santos

0454   Mirko Ilić Corp
DESIGN: Mirko Ilić, Heath Hingardner

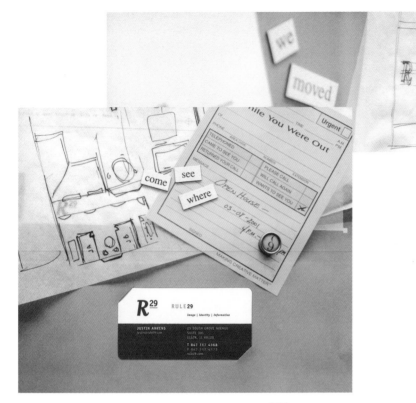

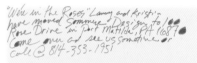

0456

0457

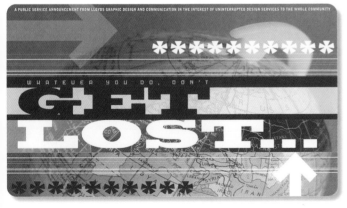

0455

| 0455 | Lloyds Graphic Design
DESIGN: Alexander Lloyd | 0456 | Rule 29
DESIGN: Justin Ahrens, Jim Boborci | 0457 | Sommese Design
DESIGN: Lanny Sommese |

0458 KBDA
DESIGN: Jamie Diersing

0459 KO création
DESIGN: Maxime Levesque

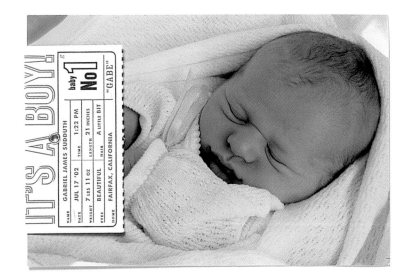

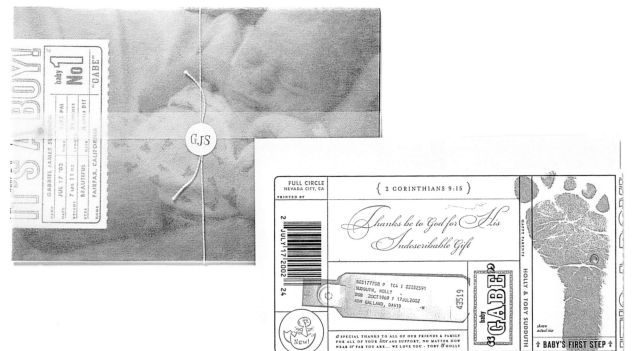

0460   Sudduth Design Co.
DESIGN: Toby Sudduth

éup

0462

Samantha Ming-Ming Roebinson
January Twentieth Two Thousand Two
Seven Pounds Eleven Ounces

JILL & PAUL ROEBINSON

Please visit www.the-roebinsons.com for photos

0463

THINKING OUTSIDE THE BOX

THE
STUBBINS
ASSOCIATES

FROM 1033 MASSACHUSETTS AVENUE

REMAINING IN THE SQUARE

0461

| 0461 | Nassar Design
DESIGN: Margarita Encomienda, Nelida Nassar | 0462 | Roundel
DESIGN: Paul Ingle | 0463 | 9Spot Monk Design Co.
DESIGN: Vivian Leung |

0465

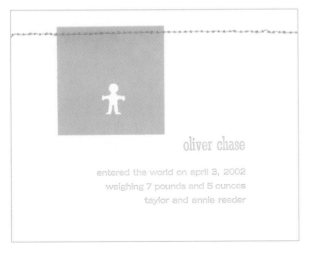

oliver chase

entered the world on april 3, 2002
weighing 7 pounds and 5 ounces
taylor and annie reeder

0464

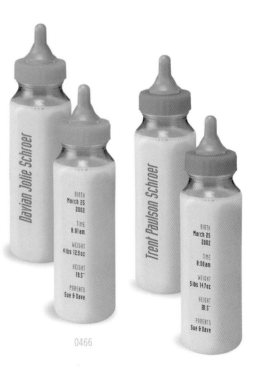

0466

| 0464 | Smudge Ink
DESIGN: Kate Saliba | 0465 | Wallace Church, Inc.
DESIGN: Stan Church | 0466 | Loudmouth Graphics
DESIGN: David Schroer |

The favor of your reply is requested by
the twenty seventh of August,
Two thousand and three

_____ will attend   _____ will not att...

_____

The honour of your presence is requested by
Mr. and Mrs. Thomas J. Donnelly
at the marriage of their daughter

—

Kelly Jean
to
Mr. Wayne E. Maw Jr.

—

son of Mr. and Mrs. Wayne E. M...
on Saturday, the twenty seventh of A...
Two thousand and three
at five o'clock in the evening
at the John Wesley United Methodist Chur...
Falmouth, Massachusetts

To have and to hold from this day forward

Sept. 27 2003

—

PLEASE SAVE THE DATE
FOR THE WEDDING OF
KELLY DONNELLY AND WAYNE MAW, JR.

INVITATION TO FOLLOW

INVITATIONS

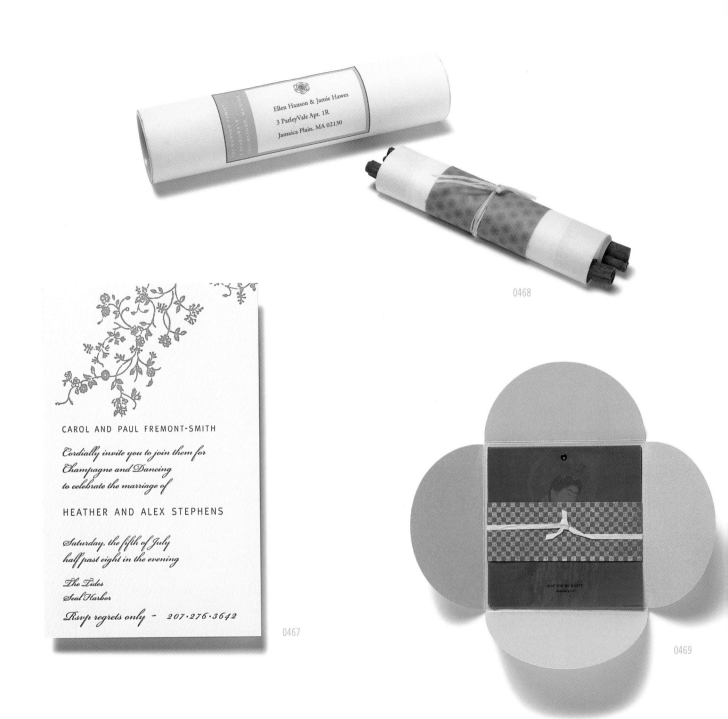

Ellen Hanson & Jamie Hawes
3 ParleyVale Apt. 1R
Jamaica Plain, MA 02130

0468

CAROL AND PAUL FREMONT-SMITH

Cordially invite you to join them for
Champagne and Dancing
to celebrate the marriage of

HEATHER AND ALEX STEPHENS

Saturday, the fifth of July
half past eight in the evening

The Tides
Seal Harbor

Rsvp regrets only - 207·276·3642

0467

0469

| 0467 | Ecrie **DESIGN:** Camilla Sorenson | 0468 | Brookline Street Design, Ltd. **DESIGN:** Heather Snyder Quinn | 0469 | Hans Design **DESIGN:** Kristin Miaso |

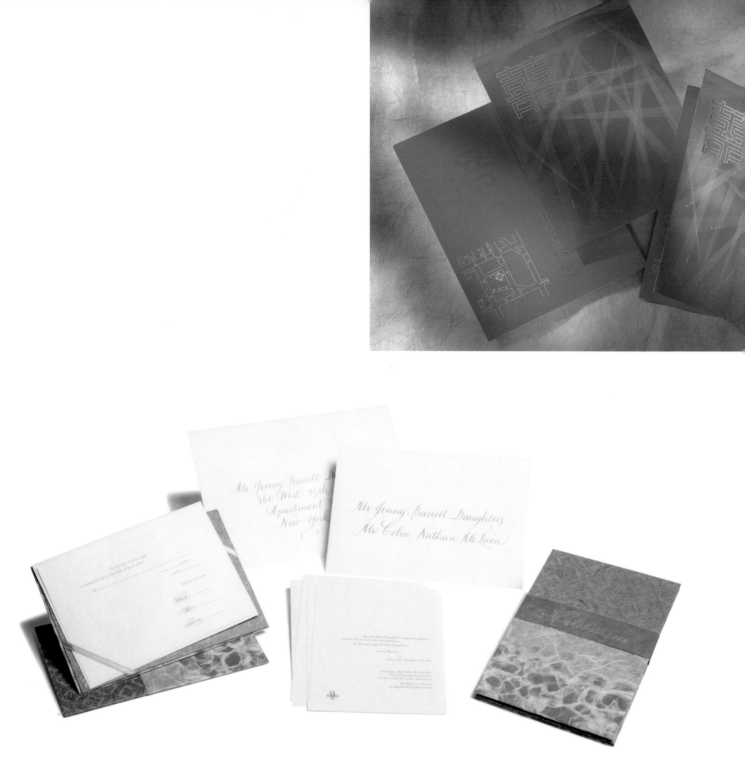

0479 Capers Cleveland Design
DESIGN: Jenny Daughters-McLain

0480 UP Creative Design & Advertising Co.
DESIGN: Javen Lin

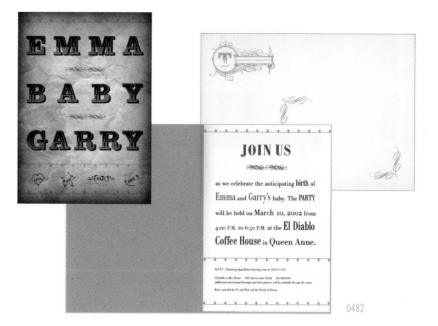

EMMA
BABY
GARRY

JOIN US

as we celebrate the anticipating birth of
Emma and Garry's baby. The PARTY
will be held on March 10, 2002 from
4:00 P.M. to 6:30 P.M. at the El Diablo
Coffee House in Queen Anne.

0482

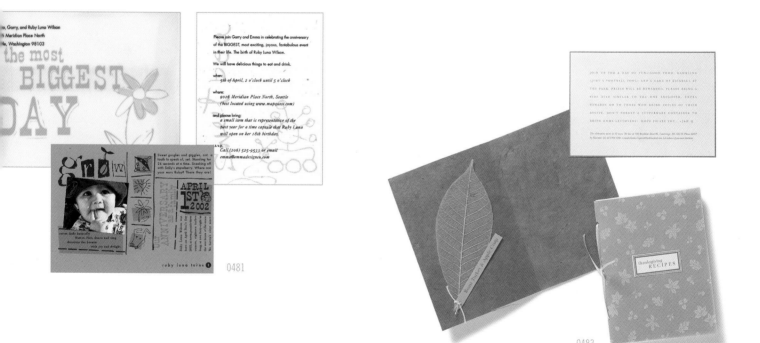

the most
BIGGEST
DAY

Please join Garry and Emma in celebrating the anniversary
of the BIGGEST, most exciting, joyous, fantabulous event
in their life. The birth of Ruby Luna Wilson.

We will have delicious things to eat and drink.

when:
5th of April, 2 o'clock until 5 o'clock

where:
9026 Meridian Place North, Seattle
(best located using www.mapquest.com)

and please bring:
a small item that is representative of the
past year for a time capsule that Ruby Luna
will open on her 18th birthday.

R.S.V.P.
Call (206) 525-9533 or email
emma@emmadesignco.com

0481

0483

0481	Emma Wilson Design Company **DESIGN:** Emma Wilson	0482	Dara Turransky Design **DESIGN:** Dara Turransky	0483	Brookline Street Design, Ltd. **DESIGN:** Heather Quinn

INVITATIONS **143**

0486

0484

0485

| 0484 | **DESIGN:** Ann Conneman | 0485 | Rick Rawlins/Work
DESIGN: Rick Rawlins | 0486 | David Carter Design
DESIGN: Donna Aldredge |

TO OUR SUMMER, SOLSTICE

JUNE 21, 2003

THANK YOU

RSVP

THE FAVOR OF REPLY IS REQUESTED BY MAY 10, 2003

M _____

will attend ___ number attending _____

will not attend ___

please see reverse side for meal selection

JUNE 21, 2003

MICHAEL & CHARLOTTE PARK
96 BALLARDVALE ROAD
ANDOVER MA 01810

0488

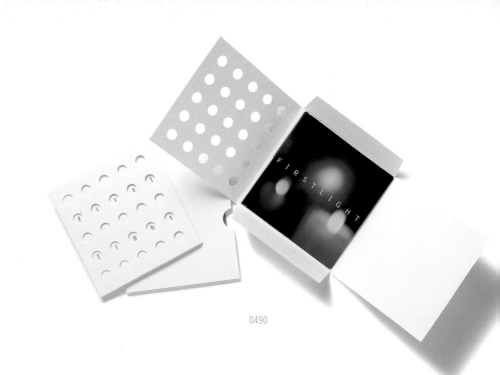

0490

0489

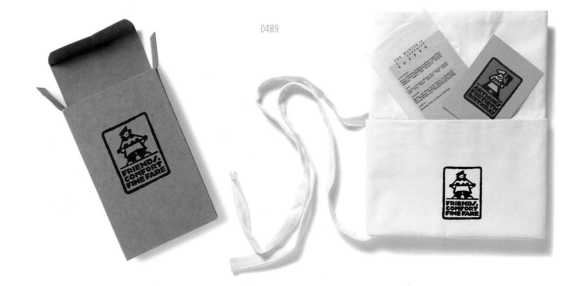

| 0488 | Michael Courtney Design
DESIGN: Michael Courtney | 0489 | Rick Rawlins/Work
DESIGN: Rick Rawlins | 0490 | Kendall Ross
DESIGN: David Kendall |

0500   Nickelodeon Creative Resources
DESIGN: Erin Blankley

0501   Kolegram Design
DESIGN: Annie Tanguay

PLACE TUNA
HERE

0503

0504

0502

| 0502 | Group 55 Marketing
DESIGN: Courtney Heisel | 0503 | Wallace Church, Inc.
DESIGN: Laurence Haggerty | 0504 | plus design, inc.
DESIGN: Anita Meyer, Vivian Law |

INVITATIONS | **149**

Insight Design Communications
DESIGN: Lea Carmichael

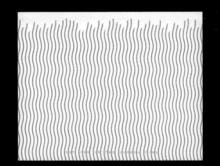

| 0515 | Wilson Harvey
DESIGN: Wai Lau | 0516 | Bandujo, Donker & Brothers
DESIGN: Carrie Dennis |

What are little boys made of?

Snips and snails
And puppy dog tails,

That's what little boys are made of.

Laura's Baby Shower ❖ Sunday, May 18, 2003

0517

0519

0518

| 0517 | **DESIGN:** Rosalia Nocerino | 0518 | Ecrie
DESIGN: Camilla Sorenson | 0519 | IE Design
DESIGN: Cya Nelson |

The little chicken is about to hatch.

A BBQ for Margaret and Damon
Jack and Jill baby shower
3:00 PM on Saturday May 4, 2002
Rain date sunday May 5, 2002
186 Brookline St., Cambridge, MA
RSVP with Sarah Jacobi 617.461.8361
Registered at babiesrus.com

0530

REGISTER TO
WIN
A FULL-SIZE SUBZERO REFRIGERATOR

showroom and fill out an entry form for a
don't have to be present to win.

The only things more memorable than our kitchens and baths?
— Our parties. —

YOU'RE INVITED

To Our 10th Anniversary Celebration & Open House

SATURDAY, JUNE 16
10 A.M. – 6 P.M.

KITCHEN & BATH GALLERY
2823 EAST DOUGLAS | WICHITA, KS 67211

Come for food, drinks and a glimpse of what your home could be.

KITCHEN
& BATH
GALLERY

0529

PROJECT READ

0531

0529 | Greteman Group
DESIGN: Garrett Fresh

0530 | Simply Put Design
DESIGN: Carrene Tracy

0531 | Gee & Chung Design
DESIGN: Earl Gee, Fani Chung

INVITATIONS **155**

0532   Sayles Graphic Design
  DESIGN: John Sayles, Som Inthalangsy

0533   **DESIGN:** Kin Cheung

THINGS TO DO

Saturday Morning Indulgences

The following are some ideas for your visit to Santa Barbara.
April is a busy time so we suggest that you make reservations prior to arrival.

LIZA 310 204 2008 | BILL 310 837 1187
SHARON (Liza's mom) 970 731 4553

0534   Special Modern Design
DESIGN: Karen Barranco

0536

0535

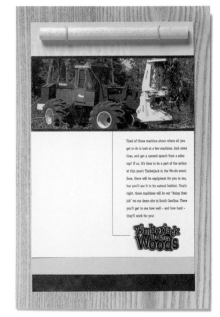

0537

| 0535 | Michael Courtney Design
DESIGN: Heidi Fanour, Michael Courtney | 0536 | ZGraphics, Ltd.
DESIGN: Renee Clark | 0537 | McCullough Creative Group
DESIGN: Roger Scholbrock |

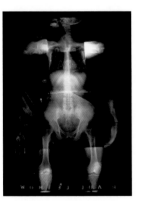

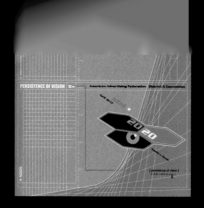

0557

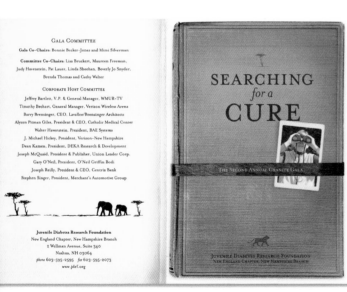

0556

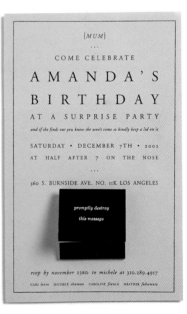

0558

| 0556 | Range
DESIGN: Steve Richard | 0557 | Hams Design
DESIGN: Renee Kae Szajna | 0558 | Design Dairy
DESIGN: H. Locascio |

0561

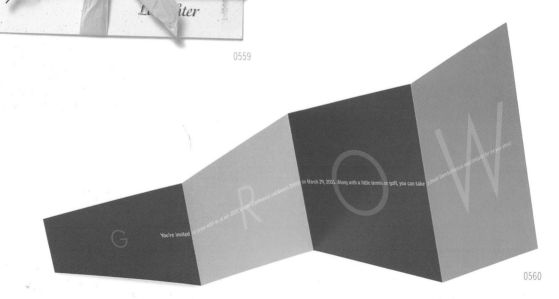

0559

0560

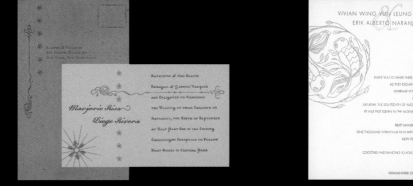

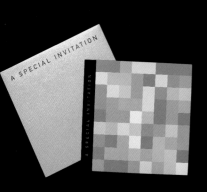

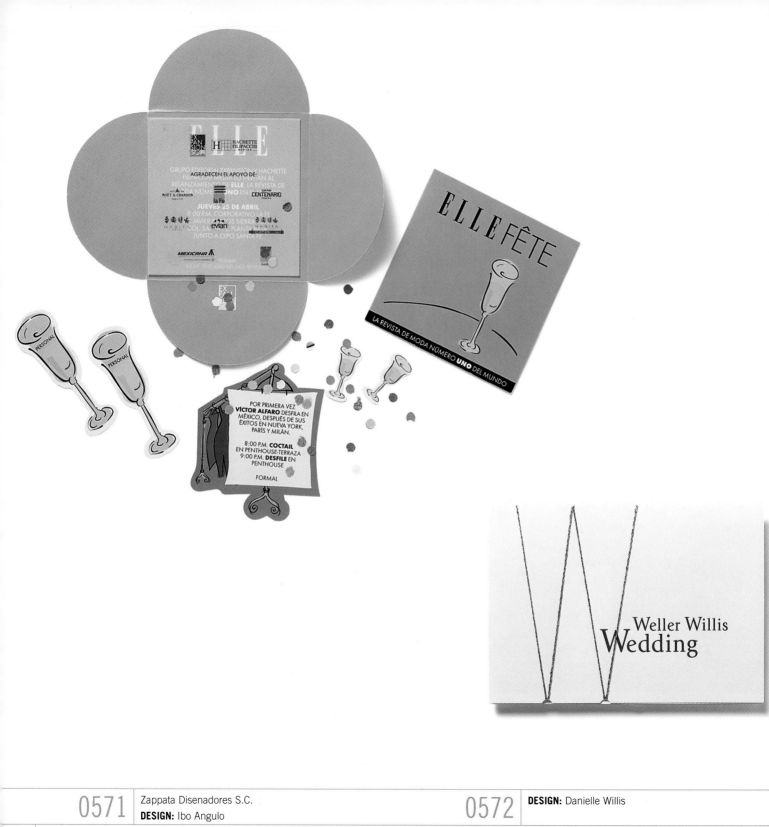

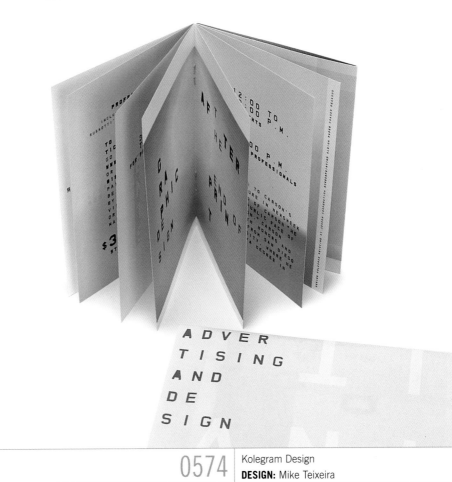

ADVER
TISING
AND
DE
SIGN

0573 | Fern Tiger Associates
DESIGN: Fern Tiger

0574 | Kolegram Design
DESIGN: Mike Teixeira

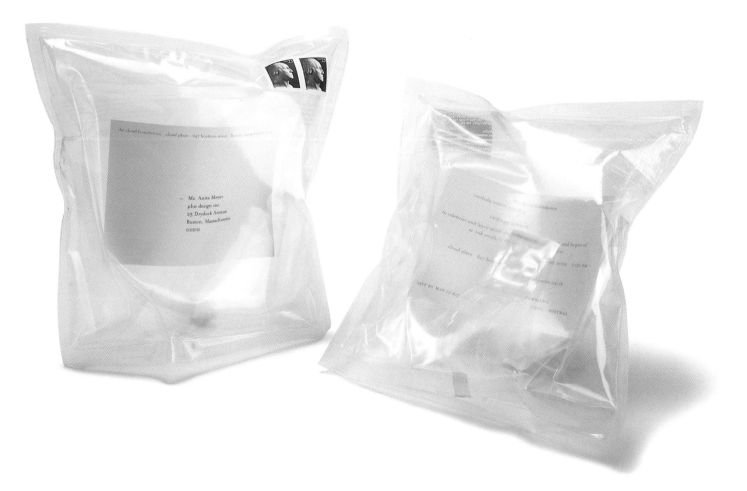

please
join
us
for
our
second
annual
wine
and
cheese
cocktail
party

saturday
december 14th
6:00 p.m.

69 crawford st.
watertown, ma
02472
(617) 926-6464

megan
and
carrie

35299 PEMBROKE AVENUE
LIVONIA, MICHIGAN 48152

Two souls With but a single thought,

Two hearts That beat as one

Mr. and Mrs. Chris Dimitriou
Mrs. Deborah Mauier
and Mr. Marcus Mauier

request the honour of your presence at the marriage of their children

KRISTI DIMITRIOU *and* CORY MAUBER

Sunday, the fourteenth of July, Two thousand and two

Three o'clock in the afternoon
St. Clement Church
Dearborn, Michigan

RECEPTION
Five o'clock in the evening
Andiamo Italia
Warren, Michigan

RSVP
The favour of a reply is requested before
the thirteenth of June

M _____

_____ will attend   _____ unable to attend

DIRECTIONS

From the Ceremony to the Reception · Turn left onto Altar Road · Turn right at stop onto service drive · Turn right on Ford Road · Bear left to turn around to go East on Ford Road (1.8 miles) · Bear right to get onto ramp with sign reading "Southfield, Fwy and M-39 N." · Follow ramp and then bear left to merge onto Southfield Fwy N. · Stay on Fwy for 7 miles · Continue on Southfield Road for 1.8 miles · Turn right onto W. 11 Mile Road · Continue on ramp at sign reading "I-696 E, Walter P. Reuther Fwy" · Go east on I-696 for 10 miles · Exit I-696 via ramp at sign reading "Exit 22 to Mound Road" · Turn left onto ramp for Mound Road North · Follow Mound Road for about 3 miles · Turn right onto E. 13 Mile Road · Andiamo Italia is on the right

0578   Grapevine
DESIGN: Karen Bartolomei

0579   **DESIGN:** Megan Cooney

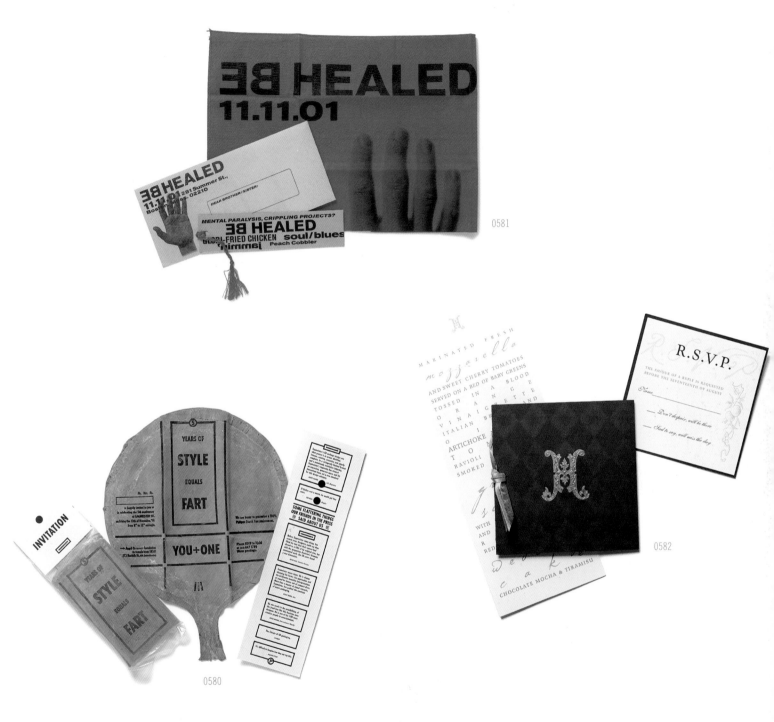

| 0580 | Sagmeister, Inc. **DESIGN:** Hjalti Karlsson | 0581 | Rick Rawlins/Work **DESIGN:** Rick Rawlins | 0582 | **DESIGN:** Jennifer Hugunin |

0584

0585

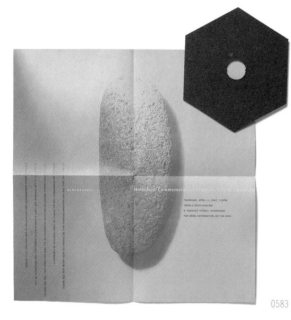

0583

| 0583 | Rick Rawlins/Work
DESIGN: Rick Rawlins | 0584 | GARISGRAFIS
DESIGN: Liza Zahir | 0585 | John Kneapler Design
DESIGN: Colleen Shea |

170 | 1,000 GREETINGS

HOLD THE DATE

INVITATION

A Hanukkah Feast and Celebration Like No Other...
And You're Invited

Auschwitz Jewish Center Foundation
36 West 44th Street, Suite 310
New York, NY 10036

0586

MAY 10 2001

SAVE THE DATE!

Boston Public Library

**McKIM BUILDING
COPLEY SQUARE**

You're due for one truly spectacular
evening at The Boston Public
Library Foundation Spring Gala
on the date indicated above.

For information, please contact
Daria McLean at the Foundation.
617.247.8980 / daria@bplf.com

0588

RESERVE TICKETS

Tickets at $100
Young Professionals Event Sponsor at $500
(Includes 2 tickets & listing in the Program Book)
(We cannot attend, but enclosed is a fully
tax-deductible contribution

Name:

Address:

Total enclosed $

Telephone:

Email:

Kindly respond by 05/01/01.
Tickets will be mailed prior to the event.
Please make checks payable to:
The Boston Public Library Foundation
700 Boylston Street, Boston, MA 02116
Credit cards accepted: MC VISA AE (circle one)
CC#

Exp.

Signature

FRIDAY
DEC. 14
7-9 PM

Juicy Temples Creative

Get your can in here!

0587

| 0586 | Mirko Ilic
DESIGN: Mirko Ilic, Heath Hindgardner | 0587 | Juicy Temples Creative
DESIGN: Klaus Heesch, Mike Fusco | 0588 | Uturn Design
DESIGN: Stephanie Zelman |

INVITATIONS 171

0589–0593

Greta Berger
DESIGN: Greta Berger

Brookline Street Design, Ltd.
DESIGN: Heather Snyder Quinn

SiSu Design
DESIGN: Jennifer Stucker

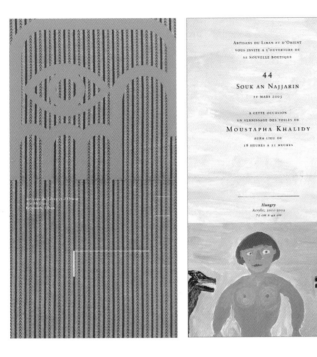

0605 Nassar Design
DESIGN: Margarita Encomienda, Nelida Nassar

0606 Donegan Creative
DESIGN: Lorraine Donegan

0608

0607

0609

| 0607 | Brookline Street Design, Ltd.
DESIGN: Heather Snyder Quinn | 0608 | Sayles Graphic Design
DESIGN: John Sayles, Som Inthalangsy | 0609 | Grapevine
DESIGN: Karen Bartolomei |

0611   Kolegram Design
DESIGN: Annie Tanguay, Gontran Blais

0612   Anderson Thomas Design
DESIGN: Jay Smith

0614

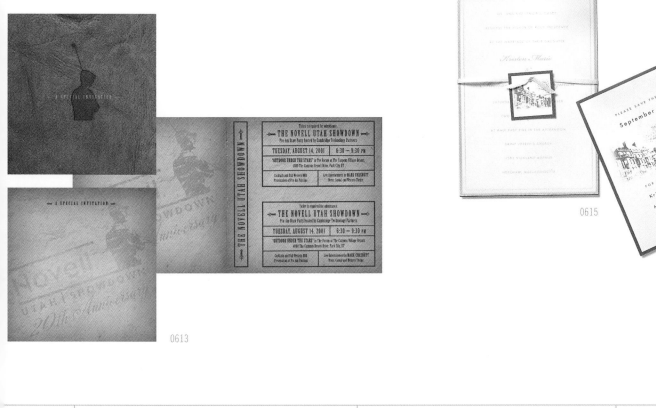

0613

0615

| 0613 | Love Communication
DESIGN: Craig Lee | 0614 | Tom Fowler, Inc.
DESIGN: Thomas G. Fowler, Karl S. Maruyama | 0615 | Brookline Street Design, Ltd.
DESIGN: Heather Snyder Quinn |

| 0625 | R2 design
DESIGN: Lize Defossez Ramalho, Artur Rebelo | 0626 | Cahoots
DESIGN: Michael Bouchard |

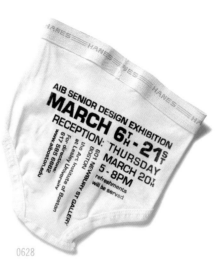

0628

0627

0629

0627   Rick Rawlins/Work
DESIGN: Rick Rawlins

0628   **DESIGN:** Prank

0629   Pernsteiner Creative Group,
DESIGN: Andy Hauck

182 | 1,000 GREETINGS

0631 Kolegram Design
DESIGN: Jean-Francois Plante

0632 Brookline Street Design, Ltd.
DESIGN: Heather Snyder Quinn

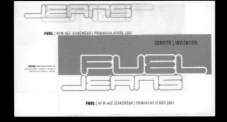

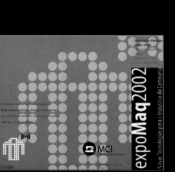

0642

0644

0642	AKA Design	0643	Gutierrez Design Associates	0644	John Kneapler Design
	DESIGN: Stacy Lanier		**DESIGN:** Jeannette Gutierrez		**DESIGN:** Niccole White

186 | 1,000 GREETINGS

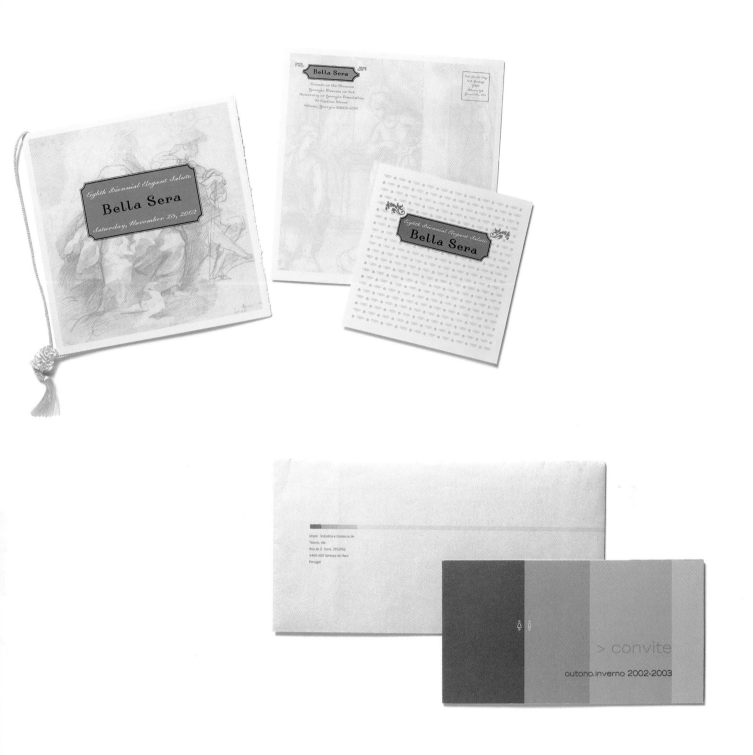

0645	Garfinkel Design	0646	MA & Associados
	DESIGN: Wendy Garfinkel-Gold		**DESIGN:** Mario Aurelio

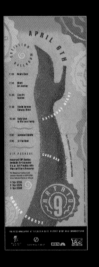

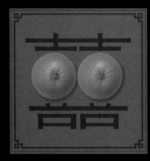

Established in
1974, the Parents
Information Centre (PIC)
is a Trust and Society aiming
at the advancement of knowledge,
education and culture. It has
felicitated a number of creative persons
in the field of drama and child education.
In the year 1997 PIC established an award
named **Navonmesha Puraskara**. The award
is to be given once a year and is of Rs. 51,000/-.

The idea behind the award is to recognise
creative persons; especially, *(though not
exclusively)* comparatively younger persons,
who have shown promise and have made a
mark in their field. This, the PIC hopes, will,
ant stage
t degree
eavours.
omoting
clusively),

हमारी पूज्या

नी ज्ञानवती लाठ

री बरसी पर

र की सुयोग्य शिष्या

गायन होगा।

पात: 10 बजे

Thursday
23rd January 2003
10 AM

Gyan Manch
11, Pretoria Street, Kolkata - 700071
Phone: 22823516/5215

0656 Appropriate Design
DESIGN: Shivani and Sanjeev Bothra

0658

0657

0659

| 0657 | UP Creative Design & Advertising Co. **DESIGN:** Andy Lee | 0658 | Selbert Perkins Design **DESIGN:** Sheri Bates | 0659 | Partners in Print **DESIGN:** Ariel Janzen |

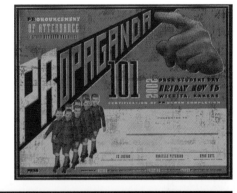

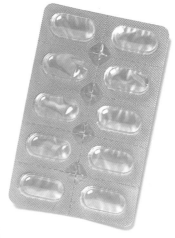

| 0662 | Rick Rawlins/Work
DESIGN: Rick Rawlins | 0663 | Watts Design
DESIGN: Peter Watts |

MR. AND MRS. ROBERT F. HUNT
105 N STREET
SOUTH BOSTON, MASSACHUSETTS
0 2 1 2 7

Rsvp

MR/MRS/MS..

ACCEPTS..
REGRETS..

BEFORE SEPTEMBER TWENTIETH

AT TWENTY MINUTES TO ELEVEN O'CLOCK
SATURDAY, THE THIRD OF AUGUST, TWO THOUSAND AND TWO

Karen Marie Bartolomei
AND
Robert Francis Hunt

EXCHANGED MARRIAGE VOWS AND WERE UNITED AS HUSBAND AND WIFE
IN MICHELANGELO'S PIAZZA DEL CAMPIDOGLIO
ROME, ITALY

THEY WILL RETURN FROM THEIR HONEYMOON IN PARIS, FRANCE
SATURDAY, THE TENTH OF AUGUST

0673   Grapevine
DESIGN: Karen Bartolomei

OUSTED

0675

0674

0676

| 0674 | UP Creative Design & Advertising Co.
DESIGN: Ben Wang | 0675 | Popcorn Initiative
DESIGN: Chris Jones, Roger Wood | 0676 | Transcend
DESIGN: Hung Q. Tran |

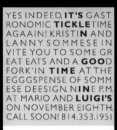

hotel information:
the following hotels are in close proximity to
the ceremony and the reception

st. regis hotel ~ two east 55th street at fifth avenue (212) 753-4500 $$$$$
...ldorf astoria ~ 301 park avenue (212) 355-3000 $$$$
...ast lexington avenue (212) 755-1200 $$$
...rand central station (212) 247-2700 $$$
...york city

we hope you will save the weekend of december 13, 2002
to join us for our wedding celebration in new york city
jennifer & timm

weekend celebration includes:
friday morning, december 13 ~ reserved acela express train car to nyc
friday evening, december 13 ~ broadway show
saturday evening, december 14 ~ wedding ceremony at st. bartholomew's church
followed by a reception at the st. regis hotel
sunday afternoon, december 15 ~ reserved acela express train car to boston

ceremony ~ st. bartholomew's church ~ 109 east 50th street
reception ~ st. regis hotel ~ two east 55th street at fifth avenue
cocktail reception ~ louis XVI suite
dinner & dance ~ versailles room

INVITATION TO FOLLOW

0687

Please join us
for an opening party
Friday, May 8th
at 7:00 pm
1-22-1 Ebisu ~ Shibuya-ku, Tokyo
Tel 5475 5291

SARA AND KELLEY

0686

0688

| 0686 | Vrontikis Design Office DESIGN: Tammy Kim | 0687 | Grapevine DESIGN: Karen Bartolomei | 0688 | The Commissary DESIGN: Alison Charles |

With joyous hearts, your presence is hereby requested to join Scott & Tracy in a celebration of love to be held at Daniels Summit Pass, Highway 40, Heber City, Utah, located in the United States of America. Visit www.danielssummit.com for information.

0689   angryporcupine_design
DESIGN: Cheryl Roder-Quill

| 0690 | Grapevine **DESIGN:** Karen Bartolomei | 0691 | Ideas Frescas **DESIGN:** Lee Newham |

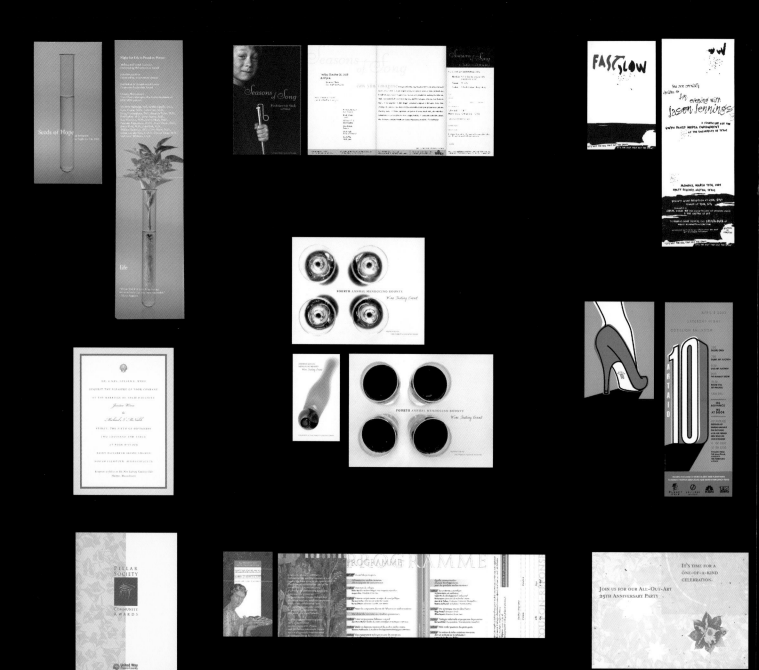

0701

L.I.F.E. Seminar
April 9-11, 2003
Santa Fe, New Mexico

0703

THERE'S A REAL SCIENCE TO THROWING A GREAT HALLOWEEN PARTY...

RATTLE YOUR BONES! IT'S HALLOWEEN!

FRIDAY, OCTOBER 25, 2002
6:30 PM TO 9:00 PM
CALIFORNIA ACADEMY OF SCIENCES
GOLDEN GATE PARK

$95 PER ADULT, FREE FOR CHILDREN.
(CHILDREN MUST BE ACCOMPANIED BY AN ADULT.)
RSVP BY OCTOBER 18, 2002
SPACE IS LIMITED, SO BE SURE TO GET YOUR REPLY IN EARLY!
RESERVATIONS WILL BE HELD AT THE DOOR.
COMPLIMENTARY VALET PARKING IN FRONT OF THE ACADEMY.
FOR INFORMATION CALL 415.750.7116.

CATERING BY DAN McCALL.
THIS EVENT BENEFITS THE ACADEMY'S EARLY CHILDHOOD EDUCATION PROGRAM.
YOUR SUPPORT ABOVE $25 PER TICKET IS TAX-DEDUCTIBLE AS ALLOWED BY LAW.

RATTLE YOUR BONES AT THE CALIFORNIA ACADEMY OF SCIENCES
11TH ANNUAL HALLOWEEN COSTUME PARTY!

FOR KIDS OF ALL AGES, IT'S AS SPOOKY —
AND AS FUN — AS HALLOWEEN GETS.
FROM THE MORRISON PLANETARIUM TO
THE STEINHART AQUARIUM AND
OUR POPULAR SKULLS EXHIBIT,
OUR SCIENTISTS ARE GEARED UP
FOR A GHOULISHLY GOOD TIME
WITH PLENTY OF CREEPY BUGS,
WEIRD FISH, AND SPINE-TINGLING STORIES
ABOUT THE NATURAL WORLD.

MAKE A MASK. GET TATTOOS.
WEAR A COSTUME. FOLLOW CLUES.
PAINT YOUR FACE. MAKE THE SCENE.
RATTLE YOUR BONES! IT'S HALLOWEEN!

0702

0701	Ecrie	0702	Alterpop	0703	Wages Design, Inc.
	DESIGN: Camilla Sorenson		**DESIGN:** Kimberly Powell		**DESIGN:** Diane Kim

0704 Simply Put Design
DESIGN: Carrene Tracy

0707

	IE Design
	DESIGN: Amy Klass, Cya Nelson

0708

	Riordon Design
	DESIGN: Sharon Pece

0709

	IE Design
	DESIGN: Cya Nelson

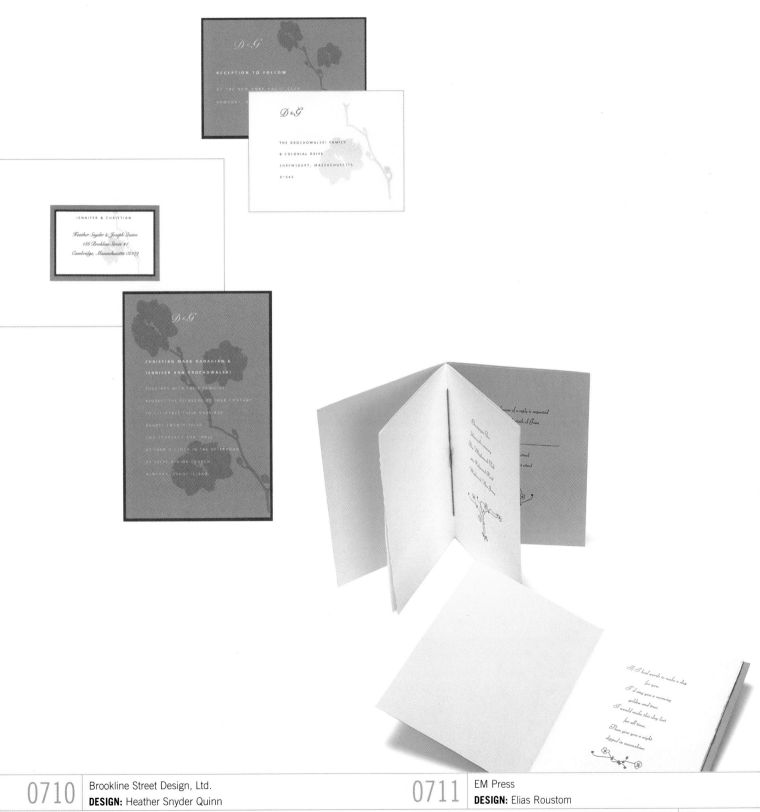

0710   Brookline Street Design, Ltd.
       DESIGN: Heather Snyder Quinn

0711   EM Press
       DESIGN: Elias Roustom

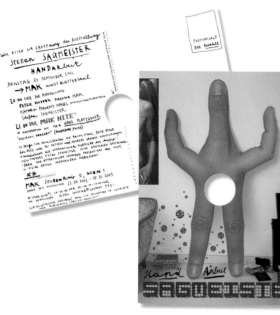

0714

0715

0716

| 0714 | Sagmeister Inc.
DESIGN: Matthias Arnstberger | 0715 | AKA Dsign
DESIGN: Amy Ray | 0716 | Gutierrez Design Associates
DESIGN: Jeannette Gutierrez |

INVITATIONS **207**

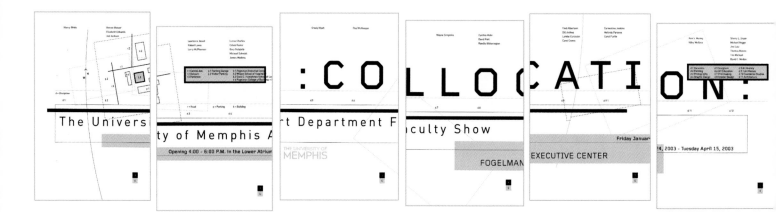

The Commissary
DESIGN: Lucas Charles

We hope you will be able to join us
ON OUR WEDDING DAY
September 13, 2003
AT THE JACKSON HOUSE INN
Woodstock, Vermont

ASHLEY BAXTER & ERIC BARTLETT
invitation to follow

Hotel information

WOODSTOCK INN AND RESORT..........$250.00*
Fourteen The Green, Woodstock
802.457.1100 toll free 800.448.7900 www.woodstockinn.com

THE SHIRE MOTEL $90-150*
46 Pleasant Street, Woodstock
802.457.9211 www.shiremotel.com

FOR MORE INFORMATION
Visit www.woodstockst.com or call toll free 888.496.6378 for availability

* To receive the special room rates listed above, please mention the Baxter/Bartlett Wedding
when making your reservations

ASHLEY
&
ERIC

WAYZGOOSE

WAYZGOOSE

| 0718 | Rick Rawlins/Work **DESIGN:** Rick Rawlins, Manuel Ortega | 0719 | Grapevine **DESIGN:** Karen Bartolomei |

0720   Bruketa & Zinic
DESIGN: Davor Bruketa, Nikola Zinic

0721   Greteman Group
DESIGN: Craig Tomson

0723

0722

0724

 R2 design
DESIGN: Liza Defossez Ramalho, Artur Rebelo

0723 Bandujo, Donker & Brothers
DESIGN: Connie Dennis

0724 **DESIGN:** Garet McIntyre

INVITATIONS 211

0725   Blue Inc.
DESIGN: Tracey Chiang, Nina Max Daly

0726   Barbara Brown Marketing & Design
DESIGN: Jon A. Leslie

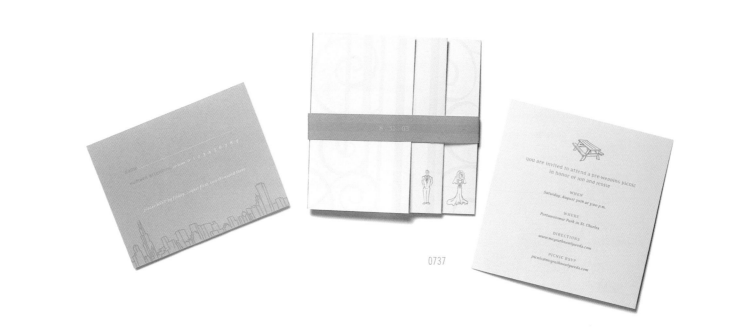

0737

0736

0738

| 0736 | Little Smiles Co.
DESIGN: Stephanie Zelman | 0737 | **DESIGN:** Jon McGrath, Jessie Bultema | 0738 | Goodesign
DESIGN: Kathryn Hammill |

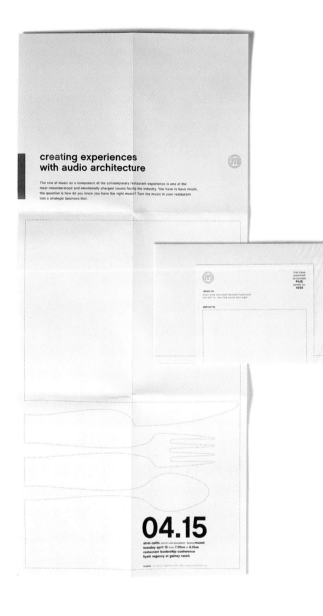

| 0741 | Zeroart Studio **DESIGN:** Jo Lo, Nicole Chu | 0742 | Double Happiness Design **DESIGN:** Adrienne Wong |

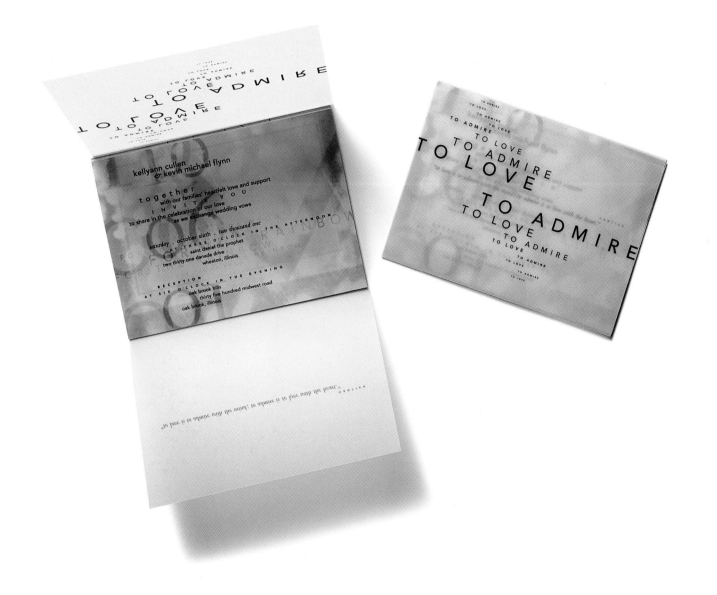

"In uns liegt der Stern unseres Glückes..."

0747

The Art Directors Club of Tulsa Presents

MIKE QUON

Graphic Designer | Illustrator

Philbrook Museum of Art
From LA to NYC
Thursday, 17 October 2002

0746

Together with their families

Jeanna DiCarlo Berman &
Stephen Daniel Reidy

invites you to share
in the joy and celeb

at six o'clock in the evening
Saturday the ninth of August
two thousand and three
at the Wequassett Inn Resort and Golf Club
Chatham, Massachusetts

Your reply is requested by July 1

AUGUST 9, 2003
Information for your stay on Cape Cod

0748

 0746   Mike Quon/Designation
DESIGN: Mike Quon

0747   Zappata Dienadores S.C.
DESIGN: Ibo Angulo

 0748   Brookline Street Design, Ltd.
DESIGN: Heather Snyder Quinn

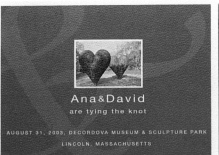

Ana&David
are tying the knot

AUGUST 31, 2003, DeCORDOVA MUSEUM & SCULPTURE PARK
LINCOLN, MASSACHUSETTS

Kindly respond by July 18, 2003

We look forward to celebrating with you

Please indicate the preferred choice of entrée for each guest

#_____Filet of Beef   #_____Grilled Native Swordfish

Randy & Marshall Davis
Ann & Martin Silverman
invite you to celebrate
the wedding
of their children

Ana & David

Sunday, August 31, 2003
six thirty in the evening

DeCordova Museum & Sculpture Park
Lincoln, Massachusetts

Dinner & Dancing to Follow

RANDY & MARSHALL DAVIS
34 CONCORD STREET
NEEDHAM, MA 02494

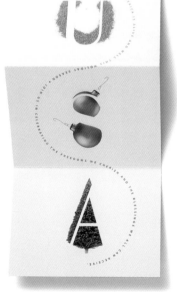

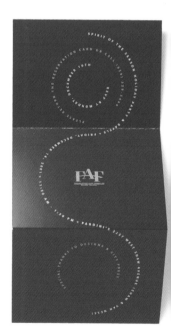

0749   Brookline Street Design, Ltd.
        DESIGN: Heather Snyder Quinn

0750   Design 5
        DESIGN: Ron Nikkel

"When you hold my hand I understand the magic
that you do. You're my dream come true."

PLEASE JOIN US WHEN OUR SON

ANDREW SPENCER

IS CALLED TO THE TORAH

SATURDAY, THE THIRTY-FIRST OF MAY
TWO THOUSAND AND THREE
AT TEN-THIRTY IN THE MORNING
CHELSEA PIERS ~ PIER SIXTY
NEW YORK, NEW YORK

LUNCHEON WILL FOLLOW SERVICE

LEIGH & CHARLES MERINOFF

0753   **DESIGN:** Sayre Gaydos

0754   Refinery Design Company
DESIGN: Julie Schmalz

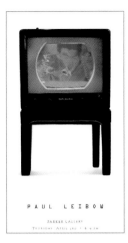

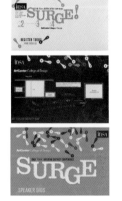

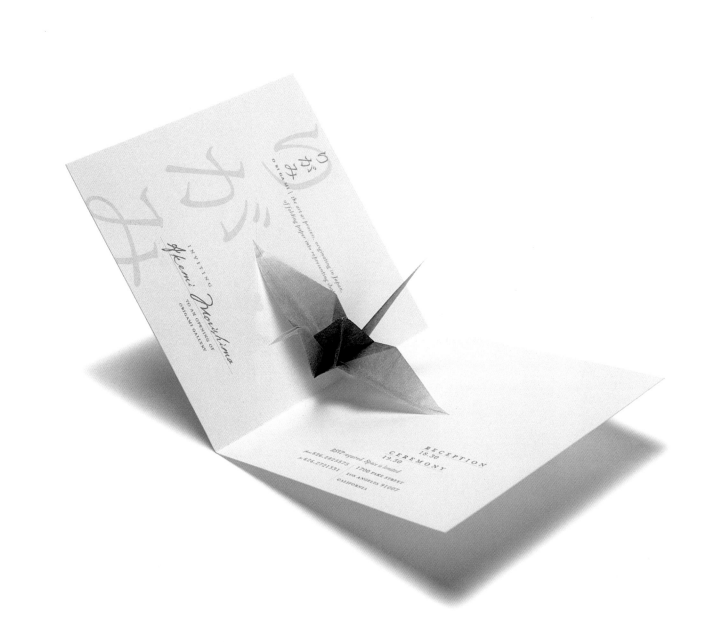

0764 Art Center College of Design
DESIGN: Triana The

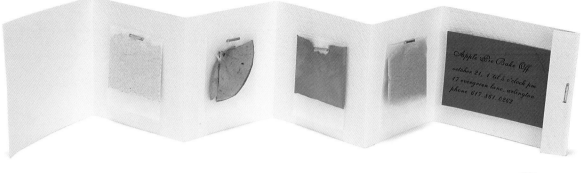

0770

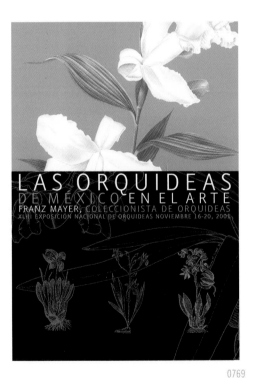

0769

0771

| 0769 | Burgeff Co.
DESIGN: Patride Burgeff | 0770 | **DESIGN:** Ann Conneman | 0771 | Rick Rawlins/Work
DESIGN: Rick Rawlins |

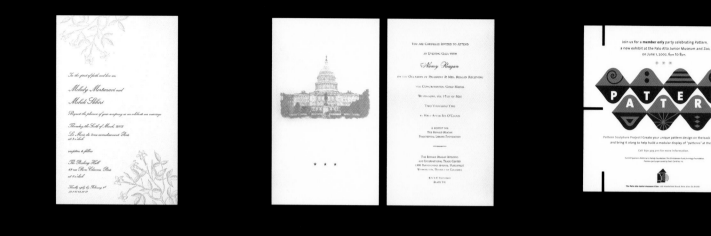

A
glorious
day of
muchness,
merriment
and mayhem

0781   Christina Blankenship
DESIGN: Christina Blankenship

0782   Simply Put Design
DESIGN: Carrene Tracy

0783   Concrete, Chicago
DESIGN: Jilly Simons, Regan Todd

INVITATIONS **229**

stavros is turning 40

come celebrate with cocktails & hors d'oevres

and music by kid capri thursday march 4th @ 9 at morton's

rsvp
margaret maldonado
(310) 535-6145

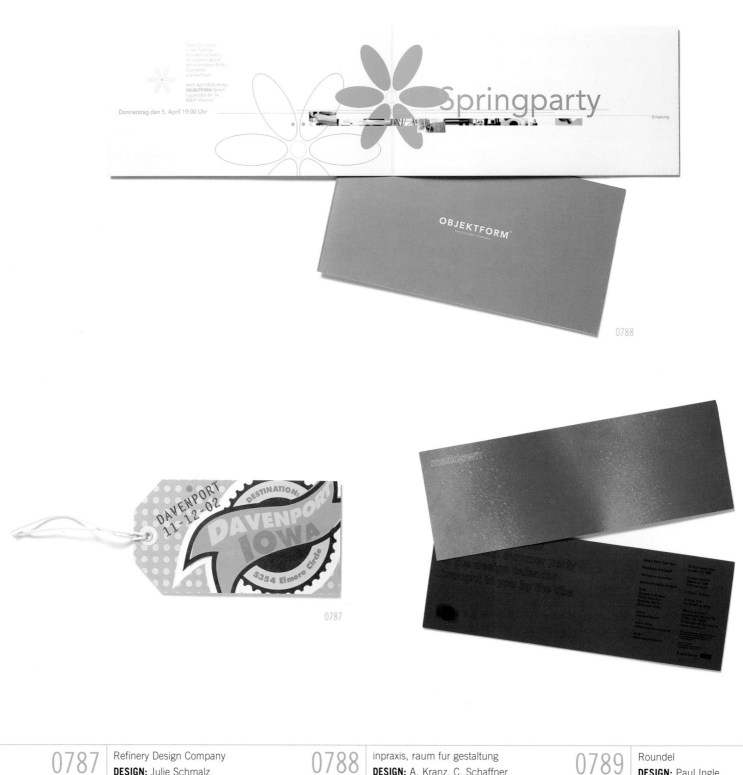

| 0787 | Refinery Design Company
DESIGN: Julie Schmalz | 0788 | inpraxis, raum fur gestaltung
DESIGN: A. Kranz, C. Schaffner | 0789 | Roundel
DESIGN: Paul Ingle |

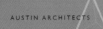

the PRACTICAL MagicBall 2003

0803

RÉPONSE

0801

Please join us in San Francisco...

0802

| 0801 | KO création
DESIGN: Dennis Dulude | 0802 | Gutierrez Design Associates
DESIGN: Jeannette Gutierrez | 0803 | Russell Design
DESIGN: Laura Ploszaj |

| 0804 | Grapevine
DESIGN: Karen Bartolomei | 0805 | Grapevine
DESIGN: Karen Bartolomei |

Michael Ray Schmalz Jr.
son of Mr. and Mrs. Michael Ray Schmalz Sr.
on Friday, the 2wenty-fifth of September
9ineteen hundred and 9inety-eight
at half after 6ix o'clock
Saint Columbkille's Church
1240 Rush Street
Dubuque, Iowa
J H
M S

0806 Refinery Design Company
DESIGN: Mike Schmalz

0807

0809

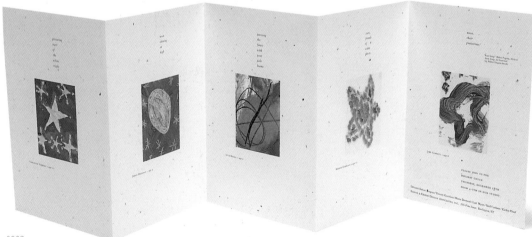

0808

| 0807 | Milk Row Studio/Press
DESIGN: Keith D. Cross | 0808 | Kehoe & Kehoe Design Associates
DESIGN: Lori Myers | 0809 | Wages Design, Inc.
DESIGN: Matthew Taylor |

238 | 1,000 GREETINGS

0819   Riordon Design
DESIGN: Cori Hellard, Tim Warnock

0824	Becker Design **DESIGN:** Neil Becker	0825	Yee-Ping Cho Design **DESIGN:** Yee-Ping Cho	0826	Vrontikis Design Office **DESIGN:** Kim Sage

INVITATIONS **243**

0827 Pure Imagination Studios
DESIGN: Josh Williams

0828 Chen Design Associates
DESIGN: Max Spector

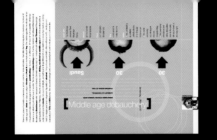

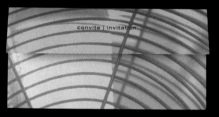

AMANDA + SCOTT

0841

Once there was a beautiful, happy place called "Detroit: City of Trees."

You are cordially invited...

But time went by. The city grew. Highways widened and many trees disappeared

...Detroit was founded

The Greening of Detroit

The Greening of Detroit
19th Anniversary
Celebration

0840

⊛ COME OVER ⊛
FOR A *really* COZY SUPPER
SATURDAY FEBRUARY THIRD, 2001
AT 8 O'CLOCK IN THE EVENING
at jennifer's house
1530 NORTH CURSON AVENUE, LOS ANGELES

WHAT'S YOUR PLEASURE?
FISH STICKS?
or
CHICKEN POT PIE?

PLEASE LEAVE IT WHEN YOU RSVP TO 323.878.2540

0842

| 0840 | Gutierrez Design Associates
DESIGN: Jeannette Gutierrez | 0841 | The Commissary
DESIGN: Alison Charles | 0842 | Design Dairy
DESIGN: H. Locascio |

0843   Grapevine
DESIGN: Karen Bortolomei

0845

0844

0846

| 0844 | Brookline Street Design, Ltd.
DESIGN: Heather Snyder Quinn | 0845 | Viñas Design
DESIGN: Jaime Viñas | 0846 | Grapevine
DESIGN: Karen Bartolomei |

ANNIE TAYLOR & ANTON INGHAM
ARE GETTING HITCHED!

SAVE THE DATE

WE ARE GETTING MARRIED
AUGUST 31ST 2002, NYC.

PLEASE JOIN US!

coffee
and
chocolate
party
2002

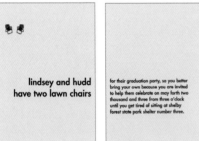

lindsey and hudd
have two lawn chairs

for their graduation party, so you better
bring your own because you are invited
to help them celebrate on may forth two
thousand and three from three o'clock
until you get tired of sitting at shelby
forest state park shelter number three.

EXPOSED!

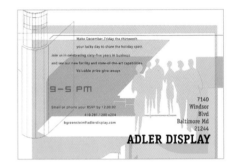

ADLER DISPLAY

0857

0856

With your help, 30 young stars will be discovered next summer.

On behalf of Los Alamos National Bank,
you are invited to a cocktails and dinner event benefiting

THE SUMMER SCIENCE PROGRAM

Saturday, October 19, 6 p.m.
Inn at Loretto, 211 Old Santa Fe Trail
Santa Fe, New Mexico

Please RSVP to Linda Dissinger
(662-1037) by October 14.

0858

| 0856 | Free Association
DESIGN: Jason Fairchild | 0857 | Juicy Temples Creative
DESIGN: Klaus Heesch | 0858 | Rick Johnson & Company
DESIGN: Tim McGrath |

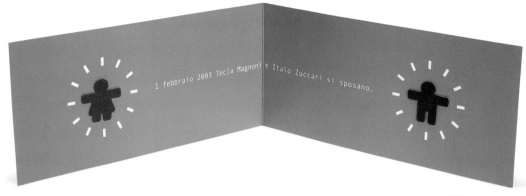

0860

0859

0861

| 0859 | **DESIGN:** Maren Bottger | 0860 | INOX Design
DESIGN: Masa Magnoni | 0861 | **DESIGN:** Laura Ploszaj |

| 0862 | UP Creative Design & Advertising Co.
DESIGN: Ben Wang | 0863 | Wages Design, Inc.
DESIGN: Joanna Tak |

0864   Rule29
DESIGN: Justin Ahrens, Jon McGrath

0865   Visual Dialogue
DESIGN: Fritz Klaetke

SELF-PROMOTION

0875	Love Communication **DESIGN:** Preston Wood	0876	That's Nice, LLC **DESIGN:** David Phan, Scott Robertson, Elan Harris

0877

0878

0879

| 0877 | Samata Mason
DESIGN: Lynne Nagel | 0878 | **DESIGN:** Stacey Bakaj | 0879 | BLACKCOFFEE
DESIGN: Mark Gallagher, Laura Savard |

SELF-PROMOTION **259**

man mß sparn wo ma knn

0889   Kim Baer
DESIGN: Liz Burrill

890

891

89[?]

0890	Chen Design Associates **DESIGN:** Max Spector, Joshua C. Chen, Kathryn Hoffman	0891	Muzak Marketing **DESIGN:** David Eller	0892	Russell Design **DESIGN:** Julie Beard

the **sensorium** reduces the sensory inputs of touch, smell, sight and taste in order to focus on the sense of hearing. music and voice are combined within the sensorium to transport the participant to a place of pure emotion — a journey into

brand.

03.16

inter-sensory

audio architecture needs to
transcend the simple act of hearing;
it must be felt in an emotional and
powerful way —

w... 03.16

RAISE ROOF

0893

AT A TIME WHEN MANY FIRMS HAVE IMPLEMENTED
CUTBACKS, WE EMPLOYED A TASTEFUL ALTERNATIVE.

INTERN JERKY™

ALTHOUGH WE HAD BECOME QUITE ATTACHED, TO SURVIVE THE
WINTER, IT BECAME CLEAR THAT THE INTERNS HAD TO BE PUT DOWN*
THE GOOD NEWS IS THAT WE NOW HAVE MORE THAN ENOUGH TO
SHARE WITH OUR FRIENDS AND FAMILY. SO PLEASE ENJOY THIS
TOKEN OF HOLIDAY CHEER FROM THE FOLKS AT LEMLEY DESIGN.

LEMLEYNDISED

| 0893 | Greteman Group
DESIGN: James Strange, Craig Tomson | 0894 | Muzak Marketing
DESIGN: David Eller | 0895 | Lemley Design Company
DESIGN: David Lemley, Yuri Shuets |

0896

0898

0897

0896   The Point, LLC
DESIGN: Janet Fried

0897   Appropriate Design
DESIGN: Sanjeev Bothra

0898   Sayles Graphic Design
DESIGN: John Sayles, Som Inthala

264   1,000 GREETINGS

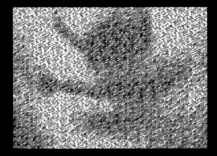

0908 Be Design
DESIGN: Eric Read

0909 BLACKCOFFEE
DESIGN: Mark Gallagher, Laura Savard

0911

0910

0912

| 0910 | Noon
DESIGN: Claudia Fung | 0911 | Mirko Ilić Corp.
DESIGN: Mirko Ilić | 0912 | Sayles Graphic Design
DESIGN: John Sayles, Som Inthalangsy |

SELF-PROMOTION **267**

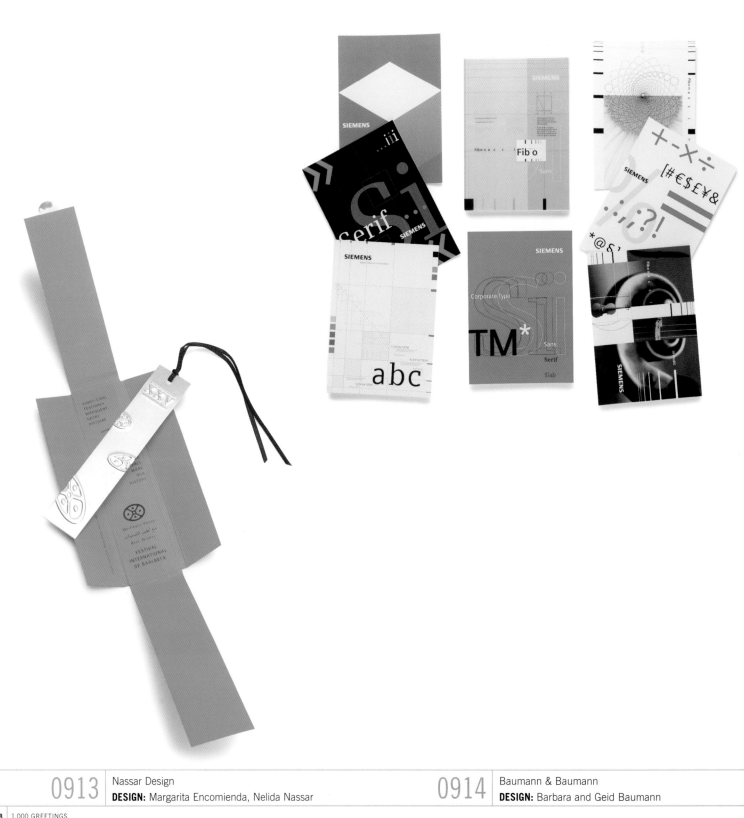

0916

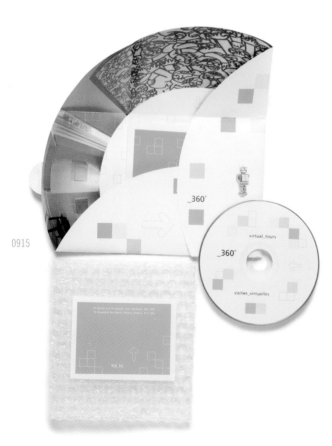

0915

0917

0915	Kolegram Design **DESIGN:** Mike Teixeira	0916	Baumann & Baumann **DESIGN:** Barbara and Geid Baumann	0917	Rick Rawlins/Work **DESIGN:** Rick Rawlins

0918

0919

| 0918 | IE Design
DESIGN: Amy Klass | 0919 | Sky Design
DESIGN: Carrie Wallace | 0920 | Red Alert Design
DESIGN: Jon Wainwright, Matt Sanderman |

270 | 1,000 GREETINGS

0921   Michael Courtney Design
DESIGN: Michael Courtney, Karen Cramer, Heidi Favour, Margaret Long, Jennifer Comer, Lauren DiRusso

0932

0931

0933

| 0931 | Egg Creatives
DESIGN: Jason Chen | 0932 | Zappata Disenadores S.C.
DESIGN: Ibo Angulo | 0933 | Michael Osborne Design
DESIGN: Michelle Regenbogen |

| 0934 | Letter Design
DESIGN: Paul Shaw | 0935 | plus design, inc.
DESIGN: Anita Meyer, Vivian Law, Karin Fickett, Kristin Hughes |

0937

JOIN THE NEW YORK YANKEES IN THEIR 100 YEARS OF BASEBALL ●

CELEBRATION

DO YOU HAVE BASEBALL ● FEVER? ITCHING FOR ● THE BOYS OF
SUMMER TO HIT THE FIELD? ARE YOU WONDERING, "WHO WILL ● TAKE
ME OUT TO THE BALL GAME?" WALLACE CHURCH WILL, AND THIS
IS HOW, IF YOU'RE IN A ● NEW YORK STATE OF MIND, GET OFF THE
BENCH AND REFER TO THE ATTACHED CALENDAR FOR A GAME DATE THAT SUITS
YOUR SCHEDULE. THE SEATS ARE GREAT TOO, RIGHT BY FIRST BASE, NOT
OUT IN ● CENTERFIELD, NOW WE'RE ● TALKIN' BASEBALL
IT'S FIRST COME, FIRST SERVE TO THE WINNINGEST TEAM ON EARTH. WITH 26
WORLD SERIES TITLES, THE YANKEES, WELL, ● WE ARE THE
CHAMPIONS. THIS CENTENNIAL SEASON CERTAINLY PROVES THAT
● DIAMONDS ARE FOREVER, SO MAKE YOUR CALL FOR THE
NEXT TIME YOU'RE IN ● NEW YORK, NEW YORK...

0936

| 0936 | Wallace Church, Inc.
DESIGN: Laurence Haggerty | 0937 | **DESIGN:** Vrontikis Design Office | 0938 | Turner Duckworth
DESIGN: Mark Waters |

A unique holiday or seasonal card is exactly what your organization needs to make that special connection with your clients, professional contacts and vendors. A custom designed card can also reinforce your organization's image and continue to build a successful graphic identity. Standard or custom sizes, large or small quantities. Let BLANK help with your holiday card this season.

Call 202.319.3120 for a design quote or visit us at www.blankInc.com

1076 Monroe Street NW Washington, DC 20010

A BLANK HOLIDAY
cards created by Graphic Design Studio BLANK

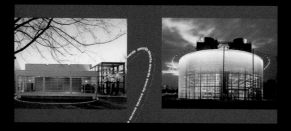

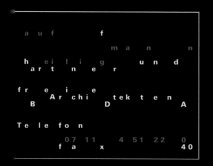

0949

0948

A PAGE IS TURnING
LIKE OUR SUN'S ARCING JoURNEY
To THE EDGE OF CHAnGE

0950

| 0948 | Trudy Cole-Zielanski Design **DESIGN:** Trudy Cole-Zielanski | 0949 | Rule 29 **DESIGN:** Justin Ahrens, Jim Boborci | 0950 | Noon **DESIGN:** Cinthia Wen |

EXPLORE   CREATE   INSPIRE

0952

0951

0953

| 0951 | **DESIGN:** Kevin Akers Design & Imagery | 0952 | Russell Design
DESIGN: Julie Beard | 0953 | Louey/Rubino Design Group
DESIGN: Robert Louey, Javier Leguiza |

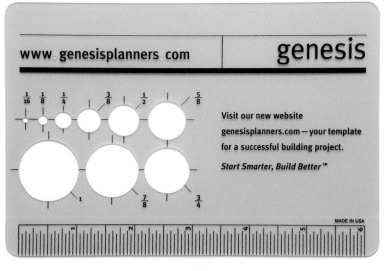

genesis

www. genesisplanners .com

| 1/16 | 1/8 | 1/4 | 3/8 | 1/2 | 5/8 |

| 1 | 7/8 | 3/4 |

Visit our new website
genesisplanners.com — your template
for a successful building project.

Start Smarter, Build Better™

MADE IN USA

1 2 3 4 5 6

0955

0954

0956

| 0954 | Group 55 Marketing
DESIGN: Jeannette Gutierrez | 0955 | Rick Rawlins/Work
DESIGN: Rick Rawlins | 0956 | Hecht Design
DESIGN: Elisa Rogers, Megan Verdugo |

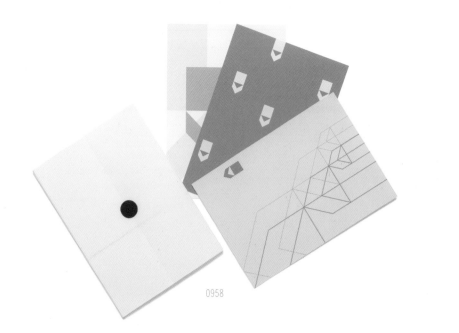

0958

0957

0959

| 0957 | Robilant & Associates **DESIGN:** Maurizio DiRobilant | 0958 | Baumann & Baumann **DESIGN:** Barbara and Geid Baumann | 0959 | Blue Inc. **DESIGN:** Tracey Chiang |

0962   Kinetik
DESIGN: Beth Clawson, Jeff Fabian, Beverley Hunter, Mike Joosse, Katie Kroener, Jackie Ratsch, Scott Rier, Sam Shelton, Jenny Skillman

0972　OrangeSeed Design
DESIGN: Damien Wolf, Phil Hoch

0973　Anvil Graphic Design, Inc.
DESIGN: Cathy Chin

0975

0974

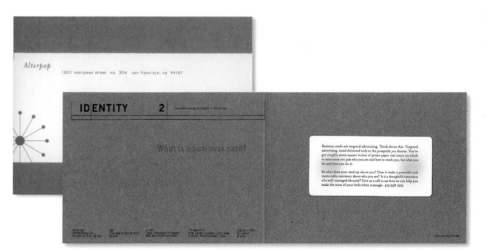

0976

0986

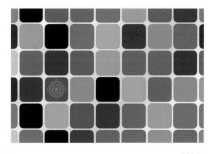

0987

0988

| 0986 | Blue Inc.
DESIGN: Tracey Chiang | 0987 | Greteman Group
DESIGN: James Strange, Craig Tomson | 0988 | DC Design
DESIGN: David Cater |

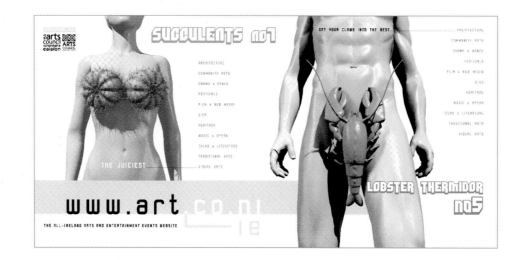

0989	Wallace Church, Inc. **DESIGN:** John Bruno	0990	Image Zoo **DESIGN:** Jamie Flint	0991	Studio J **DESIGN:** Angela Jackson

2003
A NEW ERA

Honor Awa
Honorable Men
Grand Prize
Illumination Design

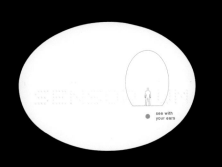

see with
your ears

OCTOBER 2002 **marks Henderson/Yates/Karls & Associates' 25th anniversary.**

We are taking this opportunity to both reflect upon our
past success, as well as look forward to an exciting future.

ascentive

ascentincentives

Subject: emptiness
Purpose: our biggest challenge
Mission: fill out according to wishes

Twinings
Speaks!

TWININGS.

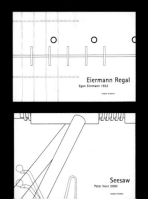

Eiermann Regal
Egon Eiermann 1932

Seesaw
Peter Horn 2000

DIRECTORY

For contact information for the following design firms, please log on to Rockport Publishers' website, www.rockpub.com.

a

Aadvert International
0779
Art Director: Heather Schulein
Designer: Heather Schulein
Client: Sennheiser USA
Software/Hardware: Mac, Quark XPress,
Adobe Photoshop

Actia
0697
Art Director: Anne-Lise Dermenghem
Designer: Anne-Lise Dermenghem
Client: Actia
Software/Hardware: Quark XPress, Adobe
Photoshop,
Adobe Illustrator
Paper/Materials: Canevas/Thibierge & Comar

Acuity, Inc.
0979
Art Director: Gail Tassell
Designers: Lori Jenkins, Deena Holland
Client: Acuity, Inc.
Software/Hardware: Adobe Illustrator,
Macromedia Flash, Mac
Paper/Materials: Silver Foil on Red Paper,
Interactive CD

ADVERSIS
0799
Art Director: Timo Wenda
Designers: Timo Wenda, Malthias Veith
Client: Malthias Veith
Software/Hardware: Quark Xpress

After Hours Creative
0152
Art Director: After Hours Creative
Designer: After Hours Creative
Client: Max & Lucy
Software/Hardware: Mac, Adobe Illustrator

0358
Art Director: After Hours Creative
Designer: After Hourse Creative
Client: Osborn Maledon
Software/Hardware: Mac, Adobe Illustrator,
Adobe Photoshop

0692
Art Director: After Hours Creative
Designer: After Hours Creative
Client: Body Positive
Software/Hardware: Mac, Adobe Photoshop

AKA Design
0642
Art Director: Stacy Lanier
Designer: Stacy Lanier
Client: McKendree College

0715
Art Director: Craig Simon
Designer: Amy Ray
Client: The Salvation Army

0755
Art Director: Craig Simon
Designer: Lauren Anderson
Client: Boys Hope Girls Hope

Alterpop
0414
Art Director: Doug Akagi
Designer: Christopher Simmons
Client: Elaine Shultz
Software/Hardware: Adobe Illustrator, Mac
Paper/Materials: 4 Pt. Krome Cote

0448
Art Director: Doug Akagi
Designer: Christopher Simmons
Client: Alterpop
Software/Hardware: Adobe Illustrator, Mac
Paper/Materials: 130 lb. Coronado Double
Thick

0702
Art Director: Dorothy Remington
Designer: Kimberly Powell
Client: California Academy of Sciences
Software/Hardware: Quark XPress, Mac
Paper/Materials: Recycled Paper, Barbed
Elastic Band,
Clear Plastic Envelope (Environmentally
Friendly), 80#
Coronado Cover (Paper)

0730
Art Director: Dorothy Remington
Designers: Todd Verlander, Kimberly Powell
Client: California Academy of Sciences
Software/Hardware: Mac, Adobe Illustrator
Paper/Materials: Sierra Paper

0976
Art Director: Doug Akagi
Designer: Christopher Simmons
Client: Alterpop
Software/Hardware: Adobe Illustrator, Mac
Paper/Materials: Chip Board-1 color offset, 1
rubber stamp, card-130 lb Coronado, 2 Color
Letterpress, Low Tac Glue

And Partners
0243
Art Director: David Schimmel
Designer: David Schimmel
Client: AOL
Software/Hardware: Quark XPress,
Adobe Illustrator
Paper/Materials: Various

0314
Art Director: David Schimmel
Designer: David Schimmel
Client: David Schimmel & Partners
Software/Hardware: Quark XPress,
Adobe Illustrator
Paper/Materials: Neenah Classic Crest

0450
Art Director: David Schimmel
Designer: David Schimmel & Sarah Hollowood
Client: HN Media & Marketing
Software/Hardware: Quark XPress,
Adobe Illustrator
Paper/Materials: Mohawk Superfine

Anderson Thomas Design
0427
Art Director: Joel Anderson
Designer: Kristi Smith
Client: Anderson Thomas Design
Software/Hardware: Mac G4, Quark XPress
Paper/Materials: Tango 10 pt C25

0491
Art Director: Roy Roper
Designer: Roy Roper
Client: Clinic for Women
Software/Hardware: Mac G4, Quark XPress,
Adobe Photoshop
Paper/Materials: Mohawk Textures

0553
Art Director: Jay Smith
Designer: Jay Smith
Client: Rocketown Youth Services
Software/Hardware: Mac 64, Quark XPress,
Adobe Illustrator
Paper/Materials: Zanders Medley-Hammer, T-
2000 and Elephant Hide, Custom Metallic Ink

0612
Art Director: Jay Smith
Designer: Jay Smith
Client: Rocketown Youth Services
Software/Hardware: Mac 64, Quark XPress,
Adobe Photoshop
Paper/Materials: Gilbert Esse

angryporcupine_design
0412
Art Director: Cheryl Roder-Quill
Designer: Cheryl Roder-Quill
Client: Lew & Kelly Wagman
Software/Hardware: Adobe Illustrator, Mac
Paper/Materials: Neenah Classic Crest,
Chartham Translucents, Metal Rim Tags

0689
Art Director: Cheryl Roder-Quill
Designer: Cheryl Roder-Quill
Client: Scott lemon & Tracy Reinders
Software/Hardware: Adobe Illustrator, Mac
Paper/Materials: Chartham Translucents, Fox
River, Confetti, Raffia

Animated Graphix & Design
0886
Art Director: Jamie Horner
Designer: Jamie Horner
Client: Mrs. Clark's Foods
Software/Hardware: Adobe Photoshop

Ann Conneman
0040, 0041
Designer: Ann Conneman
Paper/Materials: Stencilled paste paper
designs on Hahnemuhle Copperplate

0132
Designer: Ann Conneman
Paper/Materials: Hand-illustrated with
Prismacolor pencils

0134
Designer: Ann Conneman
Paper/Materials: Cromatica, chipboard,
grommets

0484
Designer: Ann Conneman
Client: Gary Miller
Software/Hardware: Printed letterpress
Paper/Materials: Silver forks, cotton thread

0744
Designer: Ann Conneman
Client: Ann Conneman/John Cameron
Software/Hardware:Printed letterpress
Paper/Materials: Kitakata japanese paper,
birch leaves, waxed linen thread, chipboard
boxes

0770
Designer: Ann Conneman
Client: Gary Miller
Paper/Materials: Flour, apples, cinnamon,
sugar, plastic bags, staples, Velke Losiny paper

Anvil Graphic Design, Inc.
0229
Art Directors: Laura Bauer, Roy Tabuma
Designers: Gary Wong, Cathy Chin
Client: Anvil
Software/Hardware: Adobe Illustrator 9.0,
Mac G4
Paper/Materials: Card-Mohawk Ultra Write
Smooth 120# Envelope-Curious Metallics
anodized

0695
Art Directors: Laura Bauer, Roy Tabuma
Designer: Cathy Chin
Client: Waldorf School
Software/Hardware: Adobe Illustrator 9.0, Mac
G4
Paper/Materials: Mohawk Superfine
Ultrasmooth 200# Cover

0761
Art Directors: Laura Bauer, Roy Tabuma
Designer: Gary Wong
Client: SFMOMA
Software/Hardware: Adobe Illustrator 9.0,
Mac G4
Paper/Materials: 100# Potlatch Scout Gloss
Cover, 29# Curious Translucent

0823
Art Directors: Laura Bauer, Roy Tabuma
Designer: Lori Rosales
Client: Junior League
Software/Hardware: Adobe Illustrator 9.0,
Mac G4
Paper/Materials: Curious Metallics, Ice Gold
Test 80#

0850
Art Directors: Laura Bauer, Roy Tabuma
Designer: Lori Rosales
Client: Peter Herz
Software/Hardware: Adobe Illustrator 9.0,
Mac G4
Paper/Materials: Curious Metallics, Anodised
Text 80lb.

0973
Art Directors: Laura Bauer, Roy Tabuma
Designer: Cathy Chin
Client: Aiga SF
Software/Hardware: Adobe Illustrator 9.0, Mac
Paper/Materials: Mohawk Superfine 130#
Cover, Ultrawhite Eggshell

Appropriate Design
0656
Art Director: Sanjeev Bothra
Designers: Shivani and Sanjeev Bothra
Client: Neerja & Mukund Lath
Software/Hardware: Adobe Photoshop,
Macromedia Freehand, PageMaker, Mac
Paper/Materials: Lucky Parchment Paper-
Yellow 100 gsm, Lofty Natural Card 370 gsm

0897
Art Director: Sanjeev Bothra
Designer: Sanjeev Bothra
Client: Appropriate Design
Software/Hardware: Manual Illustration, Adopt
Photoshop, PageMaker, Mac
Paper/Materials: TARA Hand Made Paper-Off
White & Double Ply Black, String, Beads

Art Center College of Design
0764
Art Director: Gloria Kondrup
Designer: Triana The
Client: Ori, Origami Gallery
Software/Hardware: Macromedia Freehand,
Mac
Paper/Materials: Stonehenge, Otis, Vellum,
Onion Paper

ARTiculation Group
0005
Art Director: Joseph Chan
Designers: Joseph Chan, James Ayotte
Client: ARTiculation Group
Software/Hardware: Adobe Illustrator, Adobe
Photoshop, Quark Xpress

0068, 0374
Art Director: Joseph Chan
Designers: Joseph Chan, James Ayotte
Client: WineCountry Vintners
Software/Hardware: Adobe Illustrator, Adobe
Photoshop, Quark Xpress

0180
Art Director: Joseph Chan
Designers: Joseph Chan, Wilson Lam, Helen
Ng, Karin Fukuzawa
Client: ARTiculation Group
Software/Hardware: Adobe Illustrator, Adobe
Photoshop, Quark XPress
Paper/Materials: Bravo

Artistic Announcements
0230
Art Director: K.E. Roehr
Designer: K. E. Roehr
Client: The Rockwell Group
Software/Hardware: Adobe Illustrator, Mac
Paper/Materials: Strathmore, Puritan Press,
Tru-Line Die Cutting

0559
Art Director: K. E. Roehr
Designer: K. E. Roehr
Client: Theresa & Ryan Luther
Software/Hardware: Adobe Photoshop,
Quark XPress, Mac
Paper/Materials: Raffia, Leaves, Rubber
Stamps

Asher Studio
0073
Art Director: Connie Asher
Designers: Russ Chilcoat, Gretchen Wilis
Client: Asher Studio
Software/Hardware: Quark Xpress, Adobe
Illustrator, Adobe Photoshop
Paper/Materials: Fox River Confetti, Mohawk
Options

b

Bah! Design
0396
Art Director: Neely Ashmun
Designer: Scott Herron
Client: Bah! Design
Software/Hardware: Adobe Illustrator
Paper/Materials: Color Laser Print

0550
Art Director: Neely Ashmun
Designers: Scott Herron, Rob Seale
Client: American Advertising Federation,
District Ten
Software/Hardware: Adobe Photoshop,
Quark XPress
Paper/Materials: Classic Laid

0599
Art Director: Neely Ashmun
Designers: Scott Herron, Lindsey Taylor
Client: Women & Their Work
Software/Hardware: Adobe Illustrator,
Streamline
Paper/Materials: Carnival Yellow

0633
Art Director: Neely Ashmun
Designers: Scott Herron, Rob Seale
Client: Women & Their Work
Software/Hardware: Adobe Photoshop,
Quark Xpress

0638
Art Director: Neely Ashmaun
Designer: Scott Herron
Client: Austin Shakespeare Festival
Software/Hardware: Adobe Photoshop,
Quark Xpress

0698
Art Director: Neely Ashmun
Designer: Scott Herron
Client: Gwynn David Media Endowment at VT
Software/Hardware: Adobe Illustrator
Paper/Materials: Unisource

0700
Art Director: Neely Ashmun
Designer: Scott Herron
Client: Women & Their Work
Software/Hardware: Adobe Photoshop,
Quark XPress
Paper/Materials: Confetti

0760
Art Director: Neely Ashmun
Designers: Scott Herron, Rob Seale
Client: Austin Shakespeare Festival
Software/Hardware: Adobe Photoshop,
Quark XPress
Paper/Materials: Strathmore Pastel with
Decal Edge

Bandujo, Donker & Brothers
0378
Art Director: Bob Brothers
Designers: Laura Astuto, Anne Dennis
Client: Bank of America

0516
Art Director: Robert Brothers, Jr.
Designer: Carrie Dennis
Client: Susan G. Komen Breast Cancer
Foundation

0723
Art Director: Robert Brothers, Jr.
Designer: Connie Dennis
Client: Juvenile Bipolar Research Foundation

0727
Art Director: Robert Brothers, Jr.
Designer: Laum Astuto
Client: Make-A-Wish Foundation-NJ

Barbara Brown Marketing & Design
0660
Art Director: Barbara Brown
Designer: Alicia Hoskins
Client: Alzheimers Association
Software/Hardware: Quark XPress, Mac
Paper/Materials: Proterra, Sundance,
Glama Natural

0679
Art Director: Barbara Brown
Designer: Alicia Hoskins
Client: RRPLF
Software/Hardware: Quark XPress, Mac
Paper/Materials: Starwhite Hi-Tech, Tiara

0706
Art Director: Barbara Brown
Designer: Alicia Hoskins
Client: VCMRF
Software/Hardware: Quark XPress, Mac
Paper/Materials: French Paper

0726
Art Director: Barbara Brown
Designer: Jon A. Leslie
Client: Santa Barbara Museum of Art
Software/Hardware: Quark XPress, Mac
Paper/Materials: Sappi, Glama Natural

0775
Art Director: Barbara Brown
Designer: Jon A. Leslie
Client: RRPLF
Software/Hardware: Quark XPress, Mac
Paper/Materials: Hillsdale

0851
Art Director: Barbara Brown
Designer: Carole Brooks
Client: VCMRF
Software/Hardware: Quark XPress, Mac
Paper/Materials: Precision, Glama-Natural

Baumann & Baumann
0883
Art Directors: Barbara & Geid Baumann
Designers: Barbara & Geid Baumann
Client: Brandenburg
Software/Hardware: Macromedia Freehand 10
Paper/Materials: Chromolux 700 350g

0900
Art Directors: Barbara & Geid Baumann
Designers: Barbara & Geid Baumann
Client: Auer & Weber, Muchen Slgt.
Software/Hardware: Macromedia Freehand
10.0, Adobe Photoshop 6.0
Paper/Materials: Chromolux 700/350g

0901
Art Directors: Barbara & Geid Baumann
Designers: Barbara & Geid Baumann
Client: Baumann & Baumann
Software/Hardware: Macromedia Freehand
Paper/Materials: Chromolux 700 350g

0903
Art Directors: Barbara & Geid Baumann
Designers: Barbara & Geid Baumann
Client: R & W Dental Technik, Schwabisch
Gmund
Software/Hardware: Macromedia Freehand 10.0
Paper/Materials: Chromolux 300g

0914
Art Directors: Barbara & Geid Baumann
Designers: Barbara & Geid Baumann
Client: Siemens AG, Munchen
Software/Hardware: Macromedia Freehand,
Adobe Photoshop
Paper/Materials: Chromolux 700/350g

0916
Art Directors: Barbara & Geid Baumann
Designers: Barbara & Geid Baumann
Client: Veischiedene Projecpete
Software/Hardware: Corel Draw, Pagemaker
Paper/Materials: Naturpapier

0941
Art Directors: Barbara & Geid Baumann
Designers: Barbara & Geid Baumann
Client: Kauffmann, Theilig & Partner
Software/Hardware: Macromedia Freehand 10
Paper/Materials: Chromolux 700, 300g

0958
Art Directors: Barbara & Geid Baumann
Designers: Barbara & Geid Baumann
Client: Bundesjag Bonn
Software/Hardware: Corel Draw
Paper/Materials: Naturpapier

1000
Art Directors: Barbara & Geid Baumann
Designers: Barbara & Geid Baumann
Client: Lamperte & Sudiow
Software/Hardware: Macromedia Freehand
Paper/Materials: ProfiSilk 350g

Bear Brook Design
0126
Art Director: Eileen MacAvery Kane
Designers: Amanda Whelen, Niko Niarhos
Client: Bear Brook Design
Software/Hardware: Mac, Adobe Photoshop,
Adobe Illustrator, Quark XPress
Paper/Materials: Label Stock, 80 lb. Silk Text

Becker Design
0824
Designer: Neil Becker
Client: Neil & Amy Becker
Software/Hardware: Quark XPress
Paper/Materials: Mohawk, Superfine 100#C,
Soft White, Eggshell Finish, Glama Natural
27#, Pastel Yellow

0872
Art Director: Neil Becker
Designer: Kaytee Mosher
Client: Garbs
Software/Hardware: Quark XPress, Adobe
Photoshop, Adobe Illustrator
Paper/Materials: 2 Spot PMS Metallic on
Coated Stock, Translucent Envelope

Be Design
0417
Art Director: Eric Read
Designer: Eric Read
Client: Deborah Read
Software/Hardware: Adobe Illustrator
Paper/Materials: Strathmore

0908
Art Director: Eric Read
Designer: Eric Read
Client: Deborah Read
Software/Hardware: Adobe
Paper/Materials: Strathmore

Bekaert & Leroy
0083, 0086, 0143, 0146, 0359, 0363, 0364, 0420,
0433, 0655
Art Director: Johnny Bekaert
Designer: Johnny Bekaert
Client: Kartoen Fabriek
Software/Hardware: Quark XPress, Adobe
Photoshop

Big I Ranch Design Studio
0622
Art Director: Irasema Rivera
Designer: Irasema Rivera
Client: Latina Magazine
Software/Hardware: Quark XPress, Adobe
Illustrator, Mac

Blackbird Creative Services
0478
Designer: Rosemary Campion
Client: Manhattanville College
Software/Hardware: Quark XPress, Mac
Paper/Materials: Coated Cover

BLACKCOFFEE
0043
Art Directors: Mark Gallagher, Laura Savard
Designers: Mark Gallagher, Laura Savard
Client: BLACKCOFFEE
Software/Hardware: Adobe Photoshop, Adobe
Illustrator
Paper/Materials: Curious Paper Metallic
Ionised Cover

0046
Art Director: Mark Gallagher
Designers: Mark Gallagher, Laura Savard
Client: BLACKCOFFEE
Software/Hardware: Adobe Photoshop, Adobe
Illustrator
Paper/Materials: Card-Coated White Cover
Env – Clear Plastic Envelope with Hang Tab

0251
Art Director: Laura Savard
Designers: Mark Gallagher, Laura Savard
Client: Massachusetts General Hospital
Software/Hardware: Adobe Illustrator, Mac
Paper/Materials: Card-Neenah Classic
Columns Windsor Blue/Avalanche White 120#
Duplex Cover, Envelope-Neenah Classic
Columns Avalanche White

0879
Art Directors: Mark Gallagher & Laura Savard
Designers: Mark Gallagher & Laura Savard
Client: BLACKCOFFEE
Software/Hardware: Adobe Illustrator, Mac
Paper/Materials: Burlap Sack, Silver
Grommets, Twine

0909
Art Directors: Mark Gallagher & Laura Savard
Designers: Mark Gallagher & Laura Savard
Client: BLACKCOFFEE
Software/Hardware: Adobe Illustrator, Mac
Paper/Materials: Aluminum Tin

BLANK, Inc.
0105
Art Director: Robert Kent Wilson
Designer: Danielle Willis
Client: Number Six Softwave
Software/Hardware: Adobe Illustrator, Mac G4
Paper/Materials: Finch Fine

0451
Art Director: Robert Kent Wilson
Designer: Danielle Willis
Client: Mackerel Sky Architecture
Software/Hardware: Adobe Illustrator, Mac G4
Paper/Materials: Productolith

0514
Art Director: Robert Kent Wilson
Designer: Robert Kent Wilson
Client: Ryan & Martha Wilson
Software/Hardware: Quark XPress, Mac G4
Paper/Materials: Productolith Dull

0547
Art Director: Robert Kent Wilson
Designer: Christine Dzieciolowski
Client: Kickok Warner Cole Architects
Software/Hardware: Adobe Illustrator, Adobe
Photoshop, Mac G4
Paper/Materials: Classic Columns

0939
Art Director: Robert Kent Wilson
Designer: Robert Kent Wilson, Danielle Willis,
Christine Oziecholowski
Client: BLANK, Inc.
Software/Hardware: Quark XPress, Adobe
Illustrator, Adobe Photoshop, Mac
Paper/Materials: Miscellaneous

Blue Inc.
0106
Art Director: Doreen Maddox
Designer: Nina Max Daly
Client: Self-Promotion
Software/Hardware: Mac, Quark XPress,
Adobe Illustrator

0671
Art Director: Doreen Maddox
Designer: Tracey Chiang
Client: Self-Promotion
Software/Hardware: Mac, Quark XPress,
Adobe Illustrator
Paper/Materials: 100# McCoy Matte Cover,
4 cp & Matte Aqueous Coating

0712
Art Director: Doreen Maddox
Designer: Tracey Chiang
Client: Winston Preparatory School
Software/Hardware: Mac, Quark XPress,
Adobe Illustrator
Paper/Materials: Colors Brights 24#, Envelope-
Orange, 4cp Vellum Overlay, Solution White
80# Cover Uncoated

0725
Art Director: Doreen Maddox
Designers: Tracey Chiang, Nina Max Daly
Client: Winston Preparatory School
Software/Hardware: Quark XPress, Mac,
Adobe Illustrator
Paper/Materials: 80# Porcelain Gloss Cover,
PMS Silver &
PMS 877 Red with Gloss Aqueous Coating-
Envelope-Tuxedo
Park White, 4-Bar

0869
Art Director: Doreen Maddox
Designer: Tracey Chiang
Client: Self-Promotion
Software/Hardware: Mac, Quark XPress,
Adobe Illustrator
Paper/Materials: Starwhite Vicksburg 130#
Cover, Strathmore Bright White 24#

0959
Art Director: Doreen Maddox
Designer: Tracey Chiang
Client: Self-Promotion
Software/Hardware: Mac, Quark XPress,
Adobe Illustrator
Paper/Materials: Cotton T-Shirt with Blue Logo,
Correspondence Kit (Set of 4 Original
Postcards & Blue Inc. Pen, Blue Candle, Kraft
paper Bag w/Ribbon & Blue Inc. Hang Tag

0986
Art Director: Doreen Maddox
Designer: Tracey Chiang
Client: Self-Promotion
Software/Hardware: Mac, Quark XPress,
Adobe Illustrator
Paper/Materials: Glasses with Invitational
Graphics, Mints in Stainless Tin with Corporate
Logo, Letterpress Coasters with Invitational
Graphics, "Blue Rock" Candy packaging with
Rocks (Chocolate) Packaged in a Kraft Paper
Bag, Ribbon & Tag

Bob's Your Uncle
0006, 0012, 0050, 0051, 0080, 0081, 0082, 0099,
0109, 0112, 0115, 0211, 0234, 0235, 0236, 0237,
0238, 0239, 0240, 0241, 0242, 0276, 0337, 0338,
0339
Designer: Martin Yeeles
Software/Hardware: Quark XPress, Mac
Paper/Materials: Gilbert Realm

Boelts/Stratford Associates
0647
Art Directors: Jackson Boelts, Kerry Stratford
Designer: Jennifer Jennings
Client: AZ Council for CASA
Software/Hardware: Macromedia Freehand

0927
Art Directors: Kerry Stratford, Jackson Boelts
Designer: Travis Owens
Client: Southern AZ Aids Foundation
Software/Hardware: Macromedia Freehand

Brauer Design Inc.
0140
Art Director: Bruce Erik Brauer
Designer: Bruce Erik Brauer
Client: WNBC-TV
Software/Hardware: Adobe Illustrator 10
Paper/Materials: Vellum, Silver Elastic

Brookline Street Design, Ltd.
0130
Art Director: Heather Snyder Quinn
Designer: Heather Snyder Quinn
Client: Heather Snyder Quinn
Software/Hardware: Adobe Illustrator, Quark
XPress, Mac, Adobe Photoshop
Paper/Materials: Magnet Paper, Mohawk
Superfine Soft White

0161
Art Director: Heather Snyder Quinn
Designer: Heather Snyder Quinn
Client: Jen Grochowalski
Software/Hardware: Adobe Illustrator,
Adobe Photoshop
Paper/Materials: Photo by Photojenic
Photography, Vellum Cover Stock

0164
Art Director: Heather Snyder Quinn
Designer: Heather Snyder Quinn
Client: Jeff, Kris, & Ava

0249, 0468, 0654
Art Director: Heather Snyder Quinn
Designer: Heather Snyder Quinn

0351
Art Director: Heather Snyder Quinn
Designer: Heather Snyder Quinn
Client: McDevitt Family
Software/Hardware: Adobe Photoshop,
Adobe Illustrator
Paper/Materials: Mohawk Superfine

0483
Art Director: Heather Quinn
Designer: Heather Quinn
Client: Heather Quinn
Software/Hardware: Quark XPress
Paper/Materials: Rice Paper, Ribbon

0603
Art Director: Heather Snyder Quinn
Designer: Heather Snyder Quinn
Client: Aimee Calton
Software/Hardware: Quark XPress
Paper/Materials: Mohawk Paper, Ribbon, Vellum

0607
Art Director: Heather Snyder Quinn
Designer: Heather Snyder Quinn
Client: Susan Kilroy

0615
Art Director: Heather Snyder Quinn
Designer: Heather Snyder Quinn
Client: Kristin Casey
Software/Hardware: Adobe Photoshop,
Adobe Illustrator, Mac
Paper/Materials: Mohawk

0632
Art Director: Heather Snyder Quinn
Designer: Heather Snyder Quinn
Client: Heather Snyder

0653
Art Director: Heather Snyder Quinn
Designer: Heather Snyder Quinn
Client: Jennifer Novak
Software/Hardware: Pencil, Adobe Photoshop,
Mac, Adobe Illustrator
Paper/Materials: Mohawk Superfine

0693
Art Director: Heather Snyder Quinn
Designer: Heather Snyder Quinn
Client: Jessica Winn

0710
Art Director: Heather Snyder Quinn
Designer: Heather Snyder Quinn
Client: Jennifer Grochowalski

0748
Art Director: Heather Snyder Quinn
Designer: Heather Snyder Quinn
Client: Jeanna Berman
Software/Hardware: Mac, Adobe Photoshop,
Adobe Illustrator
Paper/Materials: Strathmore Pastelle, Mam
Image Owned by Bride

0749
Art Director: Heather Snyder Quinn
Designer: Heather Snyder Quinn
Client: Ana Davis
Software/Hardware: Adobe Photoshop, Adobe
Illustrator, Mac
Paper/Materials: Strathmore Pastelle, Image
Copyright DeCordova Museum

0765
Art Director: Heather Snyder Quinn
Designer: Heather Snyder Quinn
Client: Audrey Coyle
Software/Hardware: Adobe Photoshop,
Adobe Illustrator
Paper/Materials: Pencil, Brockaway Natural
Image Provided by Bride, Unknown Source

0766
Art Director: Heather Snyder Quinn
Designer: Heather Snyder Quinn
Client: Andrea Letourneau
Software/Hardware: Adobe Photoshop,
Adobe Illustrator, Mac
Paper/Materials: Granna Grosso

0812
Art Director: Heather Snyder Quinn
Designer: Heather Snyder Quinn
Client: Jen Grochowalski

0815
Art Director: Heather Snyder Quinn
Designer: Heather Snyder Quinn
Client: Kathryn James

0844
Art Director: Heather Snyder Quinn
Designer: Heather Snyder Quinn
Client: Ellen Hanson
Software/Hardware: Adobe Illustrator,
Mac, Adobe Photoshop
Paper/Materials: Glue, Tape, Bier Paper,
Neenah Classic Laid Vellum Packets,
Flower Seeds

Bruketa & Zinic
0720
Art Directors: Davor Bruketa & Nikola Zinic
Designers: Davor Bruketa & Nikola Zinic
Client: Rina Penavic
Software/Hardware: Mac
Paper/Materials: Agripina

0994
Art Directors: Davor Bruketa, Nikola Zinic
Designers: Davor Bruketa, Nikola Zinic
Client: Bruketa & Zinic
Software/Hardware: Mac

Burgard Design
0441
Art Director: Todd Burgard
Designer: Todd Burgard
Client: Todd & Gina Burgard
Software/Hardware: Quark XPress, Adobe
Illustrator, Adobe Photoshop, Streamline
Paper/Materials: Productolith Dull, 80# 2-
Color, 1 side, PMS7436 Purple & Black

Burgeff Co.
0769
Art Director: Patrick Burgeff
Designer: Patrick Burgeff
Client: Assoc. Mexicana de Orquideas
Software/Hardware: Macromedia Freehand,
Adobe Photoshop
Paper/Materials: Couche Paper, Offset

0905
Art Director: Patrick Burgeff
Designer: Patrick Burgeff
Client: Burgeff Co.
Software/Hardware: Macromedia Freehand,
Adobe Photoshop
Paper/Materials: Sulfated Carton, Offset

0993
Art Director: Patrick Burgeff
Designer: Patrick Burgeff
Client: Guia de Disetro Mexicano
Software/Hardware: Macromedia Freehand 9.0
Paper/Materials: Sulfate Certon/Offset

C

Cahan & Associates
0810
Art Director: Bill Cahan
Designer: Gary Williams
Client: Zoe

Cahoots
0528
Art Director: Carol Lasky
Designer: Kerri Bennett
Client: Wheelock College
Software/Hardware: Quark XPress, Mac

0626
Art Director: Carol Lasky
Designer: Michael Bouchard
Client: WBUR
Software/Hardware: Adobe Illustrator, Quark
XPress, Adobe Photoshop
Paper/Materials: Sappi, McCoy

Capers Cleveland Design
0479
Art Director: Jenny Daughters-McLain
Designer: Jenny Daughters-McLain
Client: Jenny Daughters & Colin McLain
Software/Hardware: Quark XPress, Mac G3

Carolynn DeCillo
0062, 0096, 0472
Art Director: Design
Designer: Design
Client: Carolynn DeCillo
Software/Hardware: Quark XPress, Mac
Paper/Materials: Laser Paper

Cave Images, Inc
0423
Art Director: Matt Cave
Designer: Matt Cave
Client: Cave Family
Software/Hardware: Adobe Photoshop,
Quark XPress, Mac
Paper/Materials: Card Stock & Photo

0445
Art Director: Matt Cave
Designer: Matt Cave
Client: Cave Family
Software/Hardware: Adobe Photoshop,
Quark XPress, Mac
Paper/Materials: Curious Iridescent,
Curious Translucent

0449
Art Director: David Edmundson
Designer: David Edmundson
Client: Edmundson Family
Software/Hardware: Adobe Photoshop,
Quark XPress, Mac
Paper/Materials: Cover-Plastic Folders,
Paper-Xerox Paper

0470
Art Director: Matt Cave
Designer: Matt Cave
Client: Cave Family
Software/Hardware: Adobe Photoshop,
Adobe Illustrator, Quark XPress, Mac
Paper/Materials: Card Stock

CC Graphic Design
0131
Art Director: Carolyn Crowley
Designer: Carolyn Crowley
Software/Hardware: Adobe Illustrator, Mac
Paper/Materials: Chartham Translucent 40#
Clear, Stardream Quartz Cover, Cupiola Italian
Paperclips

Chen Design Associates
0828
Art Director: Joshua C. Chen
Designer: Max Spector
Client: Chen Design Associates
Software/Hardware: Adobe Illustrator, Mac 64
Paper/Materials: Starwhite Vicksburg

0890
Art Director: Joshua C. Chen
Designers: Max Spector, Joshua C. Chen,
Kathryn Hoffman
Client: Chen Design Associates
Software/Hardware: Quark XPress, Adobe
Illustrator, Mac 64
Paper/Materials: Mohawk Superfine 160 #C

Chermayeff & Geismar, Inc.
0881
Art Director: Steff Geissbuhler
Designer: Ian Perkins
Client: Chermayeff & Geismar
Software/Hardware: Adobe Photoshop

Choplogic
0014
Art Director: Walter McCord
Designer: Walter McCord
Client: Choplogic
Software/Hardware: Quark Xpress
Paper/Materials: Mohawk Superfine

0045
Art Director: Walter McCord
Designer: Walter McCord
Client: Langsford Center
Software/Hardware: Quark XPress
Paper/Materials: Mead Mark V

0117
Art Director: Walter McCord
Designer: Walter McCord
Client: Kathy Cary
Paper/Materials: Starwhite Vicksburg

0218
Art Director: Walter McCord
Designer: Walter McCord
Client: Choplogic
Software/Hardware: Quark XPress
Paper/Materials: Champion Kromekote

Christina Blankenship
0781
Art Director: Christina Blankenship
Designer: Christina Blankenship
Client: Christina Blankenship
Software/Hardware: Engraving, Litho, Quark XPress
Paper/Materials: Evanescent, Curious and Stardream Paper

Ciro Design
0756
Art Director: Joan Jung
Designer: Katrina Luong
Client: IDSA (Industrial Design Society)
Software/Hardware: Adobe Illustrator
Paper/Materials: Beckett Expressions "Eucalyptus"

Citron Vert
0341
Art Director: Corinne Fare
Designer: Francois Gervais
Client: Beauté Prestige International
Paper/Materials: Silkscreen Paper

Clearboxx Creative Studio
0375
Art Director: Holli Conger
Designer: Holli Conger
Client: Self-Promo
Software/Hardware: Adobe Illustrator 10, Mac
Paper/Materials: Color Lasers Mounted on Hand Cut Poster Board

Communication By Design
0533
Art Director: Geoff Aldridge
Designer: Kin Cheung
Client: Communication By Design
Software/Hardware: Illustrator 9.0, Photoshop 7.0, Quark XPress 4.0 (Apple Mac Platform)
Paper/Materials: 7 Colour Silkscreen on mark resistant PVC, 3 Colour litho printing on Colourplan with "Brocade" embossed surface, Wax seal stamp

Concrete, Chicago
0345
Art Director: Jilly Simons
Designers: Jilly Simons, Regan Todd
Client: Concrete, Chicago
Software/Hardware: Quark Xpress, Mac OS 9.1
Paper/Materials: Mohawk Superfine, White Eggshell 100# Cover

0773
Art Director: Jilly Simons
Designers: Jilly Simons, Regan Todd
Client: Washington University in St. Louis School of Architecture
Software/Hardware: Quark XPress, Mac OS 9.1
Paper/Materials: Finch Fine, Bright White, 80# Cover

0783
Art Director: Jilly Simons
Designers: Jilly Simons, Regan Todd
Client: Lookingglass Theatre
Software/Hardware: Quark XPress, Mac OS 9.1
Paper/Materials: Finch Fine, Bright White, 80# Cover

d

Dairy
0008, 0182, 0212, 0220, 0221, 0245, 0254, 0269, 0270, 0272, 0283, 0284, 0287, 0289, 0334, 0389, 0390, 0391, 0399
Client: Dairy
Software/Hardware: Quark Xpress

0265
Paper/Materials: Paper Bag, Vellum

Damion Hickman Design
0023
Designer: Damion Hickman
Client: Damion Hickman
Software/Hardware: Adobe Illustrator

Danielle Willis
0572
Designer: Danielle Willis
Client: Willis/Weller Wedding
Software/Hardware: Adobe Illustrator, Mac G4
Paper/Materials: Beckett Expression

Daniels Design, Inc.
0020
Art Director: Larry Daniels
Designer: Larry Daniels
Client: Daniels Design
Software/Hardware: Quark XPress, Mac
Paper/Materials: Strathmore Grandee

Dara Turransky Design
0482
Art Director: Dara Turransky
Designer: Dara Turransky
Client: Emma Wilson
Software/Hardware: Mac, Adobe Illustrator, Adobe Photoshop
Paper/Materials: French Construction Kraft Classic Crest Natural White Epson Heavy Weight Paper

David Carter Design
0077
Art Director: Ashley Barron Mattocks
Designer: Rachel Graham
Client: David Carter Design
Software/Hardware: Adobe Illustrator, Quark XPress, Mac
Paper/Materials: Phoenix Motion

0486
Art Director: Ashley Barron Mattocks
Designer: Donna Aldredge
Client: David Carter Design
Software/Hardware: Adobe Illustrator, Quark XPress, Mac
Paper/Materials: Astrolite, Classic Crest, Classic Laid

David Clark Design
0011, 0361
Designer: David Clark
Client: David Clark Design
Software/Hardware: Adobe Illustrator, Adobe Photoshop

David Salafia/Laura Farr
0487
Designers: David Salafia, Laura Farr
Client: David Salafia, Laura Farr
Software/Hardware: Quark XPress 4.0
Paper/Materials: Monadnock Dulcet 80# Cover

DC Design
0988
Designer: David Cater

Design 5
0444
Art Director: Ron Nikkel
Designer: Ron Nikkel
Client: Todd & Betsy Pigott
Software/Hardware: Adobe Illustrator, Mac
Paper/Materials: Classic Crest

0545
Art Director: Ron Nikkel
Designer: Rachel Acton
Client: Fresno Surgery Center
Software/Hardware: Adobe Illustrator, Mac

0560
Art Director: Ron Nikkel
Designer: Ron Nikkel
Client: Gottschalkes
Software/Hardware: Adobe Illustrator, Mac

0602
Art Director: Ron Nikkel
Designer: Ron Nikkel
Client: Buddy Systems
Software/Hardware: Adobe Illustrator, Mac

0694
Art Director: Ron Nikkel
Designer: Tessa Schafer
Client: United Way
Software/Hardware Adobe Illustrator, Mac
Paper/Materials: Classic Crest

0750
Art Director: Ron Nikkel
Designer: Ron Nikkel
Client: Fresno Advertising Federation
Software/Hardware: Adobe Illustrator, Mac

0757
Art Director: Ron Nikkel
Designer: Chris DuBurg
Client: United Way
Software/Hardware: Adobe Illustrator, Mac

0777
Art Director: Ron Nikkel
Designer: Chris DuBurg
Client: Fresno Ad Federation
Software/Hardware: Adobe Illustrator, Mac

Design Center
0129
Art Director: Cory Docken
Designer: Cory Docken
Client: Design Center
Software/Hardware: Macromedia Freehand

Design Dairy
0141
Designer: H. Locascio
Client: Joyce Eliason
Software/Hardware: Quark Xpress

0184
Art Director: H. Locascio
Designer: Joyce Eliason

0292
Designer: H. Locascio
Client: Humble Journey
Software/Hardware: Quark XPress
Paper/Materials: Paper, Card

0310
Designer: H. Locascio
Client: Joyce Eliason

0330
Designer: H. Locascio
Client: Shana Goldberg-Meehan
Software/Hardware: Quark XPress

0387
Designer: H. Locascio
Client: Jacki Terrell

0558
Designer: H. Locascio
Client: Carri Levin
Software/Hardware: Quark XPress
Paper/Materials: Card Stock, Matches

0784
Designer: H. Locascio
Client: Stavros

0842
Designer: H. Locascio
Client: Carri Levin
Software/Hardware: Quark XPress
Paper/Materials: Linen

d/g brussels
0372
Art Director: Brigitte Evrard
Designer: Sally Orr
Client: d/g brussels
Software/Hardware: Adobe Illustrator
Paper/Materials: Modigliani Zulu women
Bead-Working

Dig Design
0323
Art Director: Leslie Baker
Designer: Amy Decker
Client: Greenstreet Press
Software/Hardware: Adobe Illustrator
Paper/Materials: Kromkote Glass

Donegan Creative
0606
Designer: Lorraine Donegan
Client: Greg & Beckie Higgins
Software/Hardware: Mac, Quark XPress,
Adobe Illustrator, Adobe Photoshop
Paper/Materials: Japanese Rice Paper, Ivory
Linen Cover, Ivory Linen Envelopes, Silk Ribbon

Double Happiness Design
0742
Designer: Adrienne Wong

DR2
0326
Art Director: Steven D. Fleshman
Designer: Steven D. Fleshman
Client: DR2
Software/Hardware: Adobe Photoshop,
Quark XPress, Mac
Paper/Materials: Courgar Opaque Cover,
Paperboard Box, Ribbon, Bell

e

Eastern Edge Media Group
0930
Art Director: M. J. Pressley-Jones
Designer: M. J. Pressley-Jones
Client: Eastern Edge Media Group
Software/Hardware: Quark Xpress,
Adobe Photoshop
Paper/Materials: Cambric Beckett White
100# Cover

Ecrie
0467, 0685, 0735, 0836
Art Director: Camilla Sorenson
Client: Private (or Person on Invite)

0518, 0701, 0772
Art Director: Camilla Sorenson
Designer: Camilla Sorenson

Egg Creatives
0004
Art Director: Jason Chen
Designer: Jason Chen
Client: Rhea Consulting
Software/Hardware: Macromedia Freehand 10
Paper/Materials: Simli

0222
Art Director: Kevin Lee
Designer: Kevin Lee
Client: Egg Creatives
Software/Hardware: Macromedia Freehand 10,
Adobe Photoshop 6.0
Paper/Materials: Keay Kolor, White Gold

0252
Art Director: Jason Chen
Designer: Lim Choon Pin
Client: Egg Creatives
Software/Hardware: Macromedia Freehand 9.0
Paper/Materials: Art Card & Styrene

0370
Art Director: Jason Chen
Designer: Jason Chen
Client: Egg Creatives
Software/Hardware: Macromedia Freehand 10
Paper/Materials: Cryogen White

0421
Art Director: Jason Chen
Designer: Jason Chen
Client: Egg Creatives
Software/Hardware: Adobe Photoshop 6.0,
Macromedia Freehand 9.0
Paper/Materials: Beckett Enhance

0438
Art Director: Jason Chen
Designer: Jason Chen
Client: Egg Creatives
Software/Hardware: Adobe Photoshop 6.0,
Macromedia Freehand 9.0
Paper/Materials: Rives Tradition

0510
Art Director: Jason Chen
Designer: Jason Chen
Client: Warren & Janice
Software/Hardware: Adobe Photoshop 6.0,
Macromedia Freehand 9.0
Paper/Materials: Rives Design

0601
Art Director: Jason Chen Y.Z.
Designer: Jason Chen Y.Z.
Client: TD Fabrics PTE Ltd.
Software/Hardware: Macromedia 10
Paper/Materials: 250 gsm Curious Metallics,
Keay Colour Galvanized

0623
Art Director: Jason Chen
Designer: Jason Chen
Client: Singapore Academy of Law
Software/Hardware: Macromedia Freehand 10
Paper/Materials: Conqueror Dapple Cream
250 gsm

0652
Art Director: Jason Chen
Designer: Lim Choon Pin
Client: Adrian Khoo & Jeraena
Software/Hardware: Adobe Photoshop,
Macromedia Freehand 10
Paper/Materials: Conqueror Iridescent Silica
Blue 250 gsm

0931
Art Director: Jason Chen
Designer: Jason Chen
Client: Egg Creatives
Software/Hardware: Macromedia Freehand 10
Paper/Materials: Miscellaneous

Emery Vincent Design
0342
Art Director: Emery Vincent Design
Designer: Emery Vincent Design
Client: Emery Vincent Design
Software/Hardware: Mac, Adobe Illustrator
Paper/Materials: 200 gsm

0542
Art Director: Emery Vincent Design
Designer: Emery Vincent
Client: IMROC
Software/Hardware: Mac , Adobe Illustrator
Paper/Materials: 300 gsm Nordset

0969
Art Director: Emery Vincent Design
Designer: Emery Vincent Design
Client: Airport Link
Software/Hardware: Mac, Adobe Illustrator
Paper/Materials: 260 gsm Snowboard

Emma Wilson Design Company
0481
Designer: Emma Wilson
Client: Emma Wilson
Software/Hardware: Mac OS10, Macromedia
Freehand
Paper/Materials: Vellem Envelope, Fox River
Confetti Card Stock, Paper, Ink Jet-Printed

0493
Designer: Emma Wilson
Client: The Vine Building LLC
Software/Hardware: Mac OS9, Macromedia
Freehand 9.0
Paper/Materials: On Demand Printing on
80#c, Vellum Envelope

0499
Designer: Emma Wilson
Client: School of Visual Concepts
Software/Hardware: Mac OS9, Macromedia
Freehand 9.0
Paper/Materials: 80# Gloss Cover On Demand
Printing

0526
Designer: Emma Wilson
Client: Spicers Paper
Software/Hardware: Mac OS9, Macromedia
Freehand 9.0
Paper/Materials: Fraser, Synergy 110 On
Demand Printing

0620
Designer: Emma Wilson
Client: Frontier
Software/Hardware: Mac OS9, Macromedia
Freehand
Paper/Materials: 80# Gloss Rouen,
On Demand 4 c Printing

EM Press
0055, 0302
Designer: Elias Roustom

0124
Designers: Elias & Rose Roustom
Software/Hardware: Letterpress
Paper/Materials: Crayon

0525
Designer: Elias Roustom
Client: Letterpress Guild of New England

0711
Designer: Elias Roustom
Client: David Spence

energy energy design
0088, 0089
Art Directors: Jeanette Aramburu, Stacy
Guidice
Designer: Jeanette Aramburu
Client: energy energy design
Software/Hardware: Adobe Illustrator 9.0, Mac
Paper/Materials: Curious Cryogen—Chartham,
Platinum-Envelope

0225
Art Director: Leslie Guidice
Designer: Jeanette Aramburu
Client: energy energy Design
Software/Hardware: Adobe Illustrator 9.0
Paper/Materials: Curious Cryogen-Invite
Wassau-Astrobrite-Envelope

0594
Art Director: Leslie Guidice
Designers: Stacy Guidice & Jeanette Aramboru
Client: Epic Roots
Software/Hardware: Mac, Adobe Illustrator 9.0
Paper/Materials: Curious Cryogen, Invite—
Chartham, Platinum, Envelope

0929
Art Director: Leslie Guidice
Designer: Robin Garner
Client: Pal Care
Software/Hardware: Mac, Adobe Illustrator 9.0
Paper/Materials: Starwhite Vicksburgh

Erin Blankley & Vincent Maccioli
0683
Designer: Erin Blankley
Client: Isabel Pipercic
Software/Hardware: Adobe Illustrator 9.0,
Adobe Photoshop
Paper/Materials: Matte Cardstock

España Design
0413
Art Director: Cecilia España
Designer: Cecilia España
Client: Andrea Sevilla
Software/Hardware: Adobe Illustrator

0426
Art Director: Cecilia España
Designer: Cecilia España
Client: Pablo Beretta
Software/Hardware: Adobe Illustrator

f

Factor Design AG
0729
Art Director: Uwe Melichar
Client: Factor Design
Software/Hardware: Macromedia Freehand,
Mac

0811
Art Director: Uwe Melichar
Client: Self Purpose
Software/Hardware: Macromedia Freehand,
Mac

Fern Tiger Associates
0573
Art Director: Fern Tiger
Software/Hardware: Quark XPress, PC

Fiddlesticks Press
0094, 0382, 0383, 0384, 0385, 0386
Designer: Lynn Amft
Software/Hardware: Polymer Plates,
Letterpress
Paper/Materials: Stonehenge Warm White

Finished Art, Inc
0019
Art Directors: Donna Johnston, Kannex Fung
Designers: Li-Kim Goh, Marco DiCarlo, Luis
Fernandez
Client: Finished Art, Inc.
Software/Hardware: Adobe Illustrator, Adobe
Photoshop, Traditional Illustration
Paper/Materials: Gloss Card

0056
Art Directors: Donna Johnston, Kannex Fung
Designers: Barbara Dorn, Luis Fernandez,
Kannex Funk, Li-Kim Goh, Mary Jane Hasek,
David Lawson, Rachele Mock, Sutti Sahunalu,
Linda Stuart
Client: Finished Art, Inc.
Software/Hardware: Adobe Illustrator, Adobe
Photoshop, Traditional Illustration
Paper/Materials: Curious Metallic

Firebelly Design Co.
0165
Art Director: Dawn Hancock
Designer: Mikel Rosenthal
Client: Firebelly Design Co.
Software/Hardware: Adobe Illustrator 9, Mac G4
Paper/Materials: Mohawk Superfine Smooth
100#C

0665
Art Director: Dawn Hancock
Designer: Dawn Hancock
Client: Neo-Futurists' Theatre
Software/Hardware: Adobe Illustrator 9, Mac G4

0774
Art Director: Dawn Hancock
Designer: Dawn Hancock
Client: Bailiwick Repertory
Software/Hardware: Adobe Illustrator 9, Mac G4

0884
Art Director: Dawn Hancock
Designer: Dawn Hancock
Client: Ladendorf Bros.
Software/Hardware: Adobe Illustrator 9, Mac 64
Paper/Materials: Mohawk Superfine

0940
Art Director: Dawn Hancock
Designer: Mikel Rosenthal
Client: Video Machete
Software/Hardware: Adobe Illustrator 9, Mac 64

0968
Art Director: Dawn Hancock
Designer: Dawn Hancock
Client: Firebelly Design Co.
Software/Hardware: Adobe Illustrator 9, Mac 64
Paper/Materials: French (Various)

Flight Creative
0978
Art Director: Lisa Nankervis
Designers: Lisa Nankervis, Alex Fregon,
Davit Stelma
Client: Flight Creative
Software/Hardware: Adobe Illustrator 9.0,
3D Studio Max
Paper/Materials: Raleigh Sumo
300gsm/200gsm

Form Funf Bremen
0206
Art Director: Daniel Bastian
Fotografer: Daniel Bastian
Client: Form Funf
Software/Hardware: Fotolab
Paper/Materials: Fotoprint B/W

Free Association
0856
Designer: Jason Fairchild
Client: Self
Software/Hardware: XActo/Hands
Paper/Materials: Handmade paper from
Thailand/Japan

g

Garet McIntyre
0506
Client: Garet McIntyre

0724, 0734, 0814
Client: Morning Star Cafe
Software/Hardware: Quark XPress

Garfinkel Design
0645
Art Director: Wendy Garfinkel-Gold
Client: Georgia Museum of Art
Software/Hardware: Quark XPress 4.1, Mac
Paper/Materials: Mohawk Ultrafelt Softwhite
with Deckle, Mohawk Superfine Softwhite

GARISGRAFIS
0584
Art Director: Mira Melinda
Designer: Liza Zahir
Client: Nana & Novi (Wedding Invitation)
Paper/Materials: Ivory 320 gr

Gateway Arts
0562
Art Director: Dave Carlson
Designer: Gina Cusano
Client: Amgen
Software/Hardware: Macromedia
Dreamweaver, Adobe Photoshop
Paper/Materials: Online Invite

0867
Art Director: Dave Carlson
Designers: Gina Cusano, Cameron Smith
Client: Amgen
Software/Hardware: Macromedia
Dreamweaver, Adobe Photoshop
Paper/Materials: Online Invite, Printed

0870
Art Director: Dave Carlson
Designers: Gina Cusano, Cameron Smith
Client: Wellpoint
Software/Hardware: Macromedia
Dreamweaver, Adobe Illustrator, Adobe
Photoshop
Paper/Materials: Online/100# Gloss Cover

Gee & Chung Design
0531
Art Director: Earl Gee
Designers: Earl Gee, Fani Chung
Client: DCM-Doll Capital Management
Software/Hardware: Quark XPress, Adobe
Illustrator, Adobe Photoshop, Apple Power
Mac 64
Paper/Materials: Paper: Strathmore Softwhite
Wove 110# Cover
Envelope: 30# Chartham Platinum Translucent

Gervais
0032, 0181, 0213, 0231, 0275, 0282, 0285, 0381
Art Director: Francois Gervais
Designer: Francois Gervais
Client: Francois Gervais
Software/Hardware: Adobe Photoshop 6.0

Gervais/Citron Vert
0207
Art Director: Gervais/Citron Vert
Designer: Francois Gervais
Client: Beauté Prestige International
Paper/Materials: Fedrigoni

0377
Art Director: Gervais/Citron Vert
Designer: Francois Gervais
Client: Citron Vert Agency
Paper/Materials: Fedrigoni

Get Smart Design Company
0196
Art Director: Tom Culbertson
Designer: GSDC Staff
Client: Get Smart Design Company
Software/Hardware: Macromedia Freehand
Paper/Materials: Used Christmas Albums, Vinyl

Goodesign
0498
Art Director: Diane Shaw
Client: KEENA
Software/Hardware: Quark XPress
Paper/Materials: Starwhite Tiara 130lb Cover
Letterpress

0738
Art Director: Kathryn Hammill
Client: American Federation of Arts
Software/Hardware: Quark XPress
Paper/Materials: Offset, Studley Press

0791
Designer: Diane Shaw
Client: Rio Rocket Valledor & Diane Shaw
Software/Hardware: Quark XPress
Paper/Materials: Starwhite Tiara 130lb Cover
Offset-Corporate Communications

0928
Art Directors: Kathryn Hammill, Diane Shaw
Client: Goodesign
Software/Hardware: Quark XPress, Adobe
Illustrator

Grapevine
0578
Art Director: Karen Bartolomei
Designer: Karen Bartolomei
Client: Kristie Dimitriou
Software/Hardware: Adobe Illustrator, Quark
XPress, Adobe Photoshop

0609
Art Director: Karen Bartolomei
Designer: Karen Bartolomei
Client: Kathryn McCarthy & Chad Maguire
Software/Hardware: Adobe Illustrator, Quark
XPress, Adobe Photoshop

0673
Art Director: Karen Bartolomei
Designer: Karen Bartolomei
Client: Myself & My Husband
Software/Hardware: Adobe Illustrator, Quark
XPress, Adobe Photoshop

0687
Art Director: Karen Bartolomei
Designer: Karen Bartolomei
Client: Jennifer & Timm Runion (Couple)
Software/Hardware: Adobe Illustrator, Quark
XPress, Adobe Photoshop

0690
Art Director: Karen Barolomei
Designer: Karen Bartolomei
Client: Sharon Foley (Bride)
Software/Hardware: Adobe Illustrator. Quark
XPress, Adobe Photoshop

0719
Art Director: Karen Bartolomei
Designer: Karen Bartolomei
Client: Pat Baxter (Her Daughter's Wedding)
Software/Hardware: Adobe Illustrator, Quark
XPress, Adobe Photoshop

0752
Art Director: Karen Bartolomei
Designer: Karen Bartolomei
Client: Megan Murphy (Bride)
Software/Hardware: Adobe Illustrator, Quark
XPress, Adobe Photoshop

0767
Art Director: Karen Bartolomei
Designer: Karen Bartolomei
Client: Debbie Adners (Step-Mother of Bride)
Software/Hardware: Adobe Illustrator, Quark
XPress, Adobe Photoshop

0804
Art Director: Karen Bartolomei
Designer: Karen Bartolomei
Client: Lorie Hamermesh (Mother of Bride)
Software/Hardware: Adobe Illustrator, Quark
XPress, Adobe Photoshop

0805
Art Director: Karen Bartolomei
Designer: Karen Bartolomei
Client: Bridget Shea & Carl Lacey
Software/Hardware: Adobe Illustrator, Quark
XPress, Adobe Photoshop

0839
Art Director: Karen Bartolomei
Designer: Karen Bartolomei
Client: Nicki Closset (Mother of Bride)
Software/Hardware: Adobe Illustrator, Quark
XPress, Adobe Photoshop

0843
Art Director: Karen Bartolomei
Designer: Karen Bartolomei
Client: Liesi Crooker (Bride)
Software/Hardware: Adobe Illustrator, Quark
XPress, Adobe Photoshop

0846
Art Director: Karen Bartolomei
Designer: Karen Bartolomei
Client: Diana Tapper (Bride)
Software/Hardware: Adobe Illustrator, Quark
XPress, Adobe Photoshop

0983
Art Director: Karen Bartolomei
Designer: Karen Bartolomei
Client: Grapevine
Software/Hardware: Adobe Illustrator, Quark
XPress, Adobe Photoshop

Graphic Type Services
0566
Art Director: Ravit Advocat
Designer: Ravit Advocat
Client: Twinings Tea
Software/Hardware: Quark XPress, Adobe
Illustrator
Paper/Materials: 4/4 Cream Uncoated

0997
Art Director: Ravit Advocat
Designer: Ravit Advocat
Client: Twinings Tea
Software/Hardware: Quark XPress 4.1, Adobe
Photoshop
Paper/Materials: Curious Papers, Iridescent &
Confetti, Translucent Envelope, 4/4 Invite &
Foil Stamp, Silver on Envelope

graphische formgebung
0084
Art Director: Herbert Rohsiepe
Designer: Herbert Rohsiepe
Client: adesso AG
Software/Hardware: Macromedia Freehand,
Mac

0107
Art Director: Herbert Rohsiepe
Designer: Herbert Rohsiepe
Client: wp.DATA
Software/Hardware: Macromedia Freehand,
Mac

0175
Art Director: Herbert Rohsiepe
Designer: Herbert Rohsiepe
Client: adesso AG
Software/Hardware: Macromedia Freehand,
Mac
Paper/Materials: Lake Paper Motion

0325
Art Director: Herbert Rohsiepe
Designer: Herbert Rohsiepe
Client: AHG AAg
Software/Hardware: Macromedia Freehand,
Mac
Paper/Materials: Arjo Wiggins Conqueror

0527, 0874
Art Director: Herbert Rohsiepe
Designer: Herbert Rohsiepe
Client: adesso AG
Software/Hardware: Macromedia Freehand,
Mac
Paper/Materials: Arjo Wiggins Conqueror

0866
Art Director: Herbert Rohsiepe
Designer: Herbert Rohsiepe
Client: Prof. Dr. Volker Gruhn, University of
Leipzig
Software/Hardware: Macromedia Freehand, Mac
Paper/Materials: Roemerturm Precioso

0945
Designer: Herbert Rohsiepe
Client: graphische formgebung
Software/Hardware: Macromedia Freehand, Mac
Paper/Materials: Roemerturm Phoenixmotion,
Arjo Wiggins Impressions

0967
Art Director: Herbert Rohsiepe
Designer: Herbert Rohsiepe
Client: graphische formgebung
Software/Hardware: Macromedia Freehand, Mac
Paper/Materials: Arjo Wiggins Impressions

Greta Berger
0365, 0589, 0590, 0591, 0592, 0593
Designer: Greta Berger
Software/Hardware: Mac, Adobe Illustrator 8.0
Paper/Materials: Benefit 100% Recycled Snow
White

Greteman Group
0419
Art Director: James Strange
Designer: James Strange
Client: Cero's Candies
Software/Hardware: Macromedia Freehand

0529
Art Director: Sonia Greteman
Designer: Garrett Fresh
Client: Kitchen & Bath
Software/Hardware: Macromedia Freehand

0648
Art Directors: Sonia Greteman, James Strange
Designers: James Strange, Garrett Fresh
Client: Connect Care
Software/Hardware: Macromedia Freehand

0699
Art Directors: Garrett Fresh, Sonia Greteman,
Craig Tomson
Designer: Garrett Fresh
Client: Connect Care
Software/Hardware: Macromedia Freehand

0721
Art Director: Craig Tomson
Designer: Craig Tomson
Client: Mike Chance
Software/Hardware: Macromedia Freehand,
Adobe Photoshop

0838
Art Directors: Sonia Greteman, Craig Tomson
Designer: Craig Tomson
Client: Flexjet
Software/Hardware: Macromedia Freehand
Paper/Materials: Carnival Groove

0893
Art Director: James Strange
Designers: James Strange, Craig Tomson
Client: Greteman Group for Habitat for
Humanity
Software/Hardware: Macromedia Freehand

0987
Art Directors: Sonia Greteman, James Strange,
Craig Tomson
Designers: James Strange, Craig Tomson
Client: Greteman Group

Group 55 Marketing
0280
Art Director: Jeannette Gutierrez
Designer: Jeannette Gutierrez
Client: Group 55 Marketing
Software/Hardware: Macromedia Freehand 8.0,
Mac
Paper/Materials: HP Deskjet 810 Output

0388
Art Director: Jeannette Gutierrez
Client: Jeannette Gutierrez
Software/Hardware: Macromedia Freehand 8.0,
Mac
Paper/Materials: French Construction

0502
Art Director: Courtney Heisel
Designer: Courtney Heisel
Client: Stratford Place Apartments
Software/Hardware: Macromedia Freehand
8.0, Mac
Paper/Materials: 80# Cover DeltaSilk

0873
Art Director: Jeannette Gutierrez
Designer: Jeannette Gutierrez
Client: Store of Dreams
Software/Hardware: Macromedia Freehand 8.0,
Mac
Paper/Materials: 14 pt. Tango CZS

0954
Art Director: Jeannette Gutierrez
Designer: Jeannette Gutierrez
Client: Group 55 marketing
Software/Hardware: Macromedia Freehand 8.0,
Mac
Paper/Materials: Black & White Laser Output
on Fraser Genesis

Gulla Design
0397
Art Director: Steve Gulla
Designer: Steve Gulla
Client: Gulla Design
Software/Hardware: Adobe Illustrator, Mac
Paper/Materials: Coated 18 80lb Cover

0882
Art Director: Steve Gulla
Designer: Steve Gulla
Client: New York University, Office of Career
Services
Software/Hardware: Adobe Illustrator, Mac
Paper/Materials: 10 pt. Coated 2 Sides

Gunter Advertising
0492
Art Director: Sarah Grimm
Designer: Sarah Grimm
Client: Gunter Advertising
Software/Hardware: Adobe Photoshop

0497
Art Director: Sarah Grimm
Designer: Sarah Grimm
Client: Gunter Advertising
Software/Hardware: Adobe Illustrator

0549
Art Director: Sarah Grimm
Designer: Sarah Grimm
Client: Gunter Advertising
Software/Hardware: Adobe Illustrator,
Adobe Photoshop

05640564
Art Director: Bill Patton
Designer: Sarah Grimm
Client: Dean Health Plan
Software/Hardware: InDesign

Gutierrez Design Associates
0643
Art Director: Jeannette Gutierrez
Designer: Jeannette Gutierrez
Client: Ann Arbor Ad Club
Software/Hardware: Macromedia Freehand,
Mac
Paper/Materials: Century Gloss

0716, 0802
Art Director: Jeannette Gutierrez
Designer: Jeannette Gutierrez
Client: Automotive News
Software/Hardware: Macromedia Freehand 8.0,
Mac
Paper/Materials: Sappi Lustro Gloss

0840
Art Director: Jeannette Gutierrez
Designer: Jeannette Gutierrez
Client: Greening of Detroit
Software/Hardware: Macromedia Freehand 8.0,
Mac
Paper/Materials: Sappi Lustro Dull

0960
Art Director: Jeannette Gutierrez
Designer: Jeannette Gutierrez
Client: Jeannette Gutierrez
Software/Hardware: Macromedia Freehand 8.0,
Mac
Paper/Materials: Neenah Classic Crest

h

hagopian ink
0135
Art Director: Christina Hagopian
Designer: Christina Hagopian
Client: Hagopian Ink
Software/Hardware: Letterpress
Paper/Materials: Strathmore Pastell, Platen
Press 6 X 10, Etching Ink, Die

0307
Art Director: Christina Hagopian
Designer: Christina Hagopian
Client: hagopian ink
Software/Hardware: Adobe Illustrator, Mac
Paper/Materials: Carnival Colors, Summer
Eyelet, Wire Ornament Hook, Beach Sand,
Laser Printed

0401, 402, 403, 404, 405
Art Director: Christina Hagopian
Designer: Christina Hagopian
Client: Hagopian Ink
Software/Hardware: Adobe Illustrator
Paper/Materials: Hahnamuhle Copperplate,
1.00gPostcards, 300# (notecards)

Hams Design
0557
Art Director: Bill Hams
Designer: Renee Kae Szajna
Client: Valspar Corporation
Software/Hardware: Adobe Photoshop, Quark
XPress
Paper/Materials: Offset Printing, Sappi Strobe
Silk 100# Cover, Gold Grommets

Hans Design
0469
Art Director: Bill Hans
Designer: Kristin Miaso
Client: E. Cheval
Software/Hardware: Adobe Illustrator
Paper/Materials: Stardream Envelopes,
Handmade Gold Paper, Vellum, French
Construction Black, Black Grommets, Raffia Tie

0677
Art Director: Bill Hans
Designer: Kristin Miaso
Client: S. Mack
Software/Hardware: Adobe Illustrator 10,
Paper/Materials: French Construction Plotter
Paper

Hecht Design
0037
Art Director: Alice Hecht
Designer: Studio
Client: Hecht Design
Software/Hardware: Adobe Illustrator
Paper/Materials: Paper Coaster with
Letterpress

0792
Art Director: Alice Hecht
Designers: Alice Hecht, Elisa Rogers
Client: Austin Architects
Software/Hardware: Quark XPress
Paper/Materials: Mohawk Superfine

0795
Art Director: Alice Hecht
Designers: Alice Hecht, Derek George
Client: UK Architects
Software/Hardware: Quark XPress
Paper/Materials: Mohawk Superfine

0956
Art Director: Alice Hecht
Designers: Elisa Rogers, Megan Verdugo
Client: Hecht Design
Software/Hardware: Adobe Illustrator
Paper/Materials: Glass, Offset Stock

Hoffmann Angelic Design
0079
Art Director: Andrea Hoffmann
Designer: Andrea Hoffmann
Client: Hoffmann Angelic Design
Paper/Materials: Hand-Crafted Metallic Ink,
Dimensional Fabric Paint, Hand Lettering, Ivan
Angelic

0395
Art Director: Andrea Hoffmann
Designer: Andrea Hoffmann
Client: Hoffmann Angelic Design
Software/Hardware: Adobe Photoshop, Mac
Paper/Materials: Corrugated Board, Adhesive
Rhinestone

Hutchinson Associates, Inc.
0305
Art Director: Jerry Hutchinson
Designer: Jerry Hutchinson
Client: Hutchinson Associates
Software/Hardware: Mac, Quark XPress
Paper/Materials: Superfine

0424
Art Director: Jerry Hutchinson
Designer: Jerry Hutchinson
Client: Frankel/Poe
Software/Hardware: Mac, Quark XPress
Paper/Materials: Mohawk Superfine

0520
Art Director: Jerry Hutchinson
Designer: Jerry Hutchinson
Client: Kids for Kids
Software/Hardware: Mac, Quark XPress
Paper/Materials: Mohawk Spetia

i

IC Companys In-house
0250
Art Director: Vibeke Nodskov
Designer: Vibeke Nodskov
Client: IC Companys
Software/Hardware: Adobe Illustrator
Paper/Materials: Macro Gloss 270g

Ideas Frescas
0691
Art Director: Lee Newham
Designer: Lee Newham
Client: Carol Christie
Software/Hardware: Adobe Photoshop, Adobe
Illustrator, Mac

IE Design
0357
Art Director: Marcie Carson
Designers: Marcie Carson, Richard Haynie
Client: IE Design
Software/Hardware: Mac, Quark XPress,
Adobe Illustrator, Adobe Photoshop

0519
Art Director: Marcie Carson
Designer: Cya Nelson
Client: DaVita
Software/Hardware: Mac, Quark XPress,
Adobe Illustrator, Adobe Photoshop

0641
Art Director: Marcie Carson
Designer: Amy Klass
Client: Davita
Software/Hardware: Mac, Quark XPress,
Adobe Illustrator, Adobe Photoshop
Paper/Materials: Mohawk 6/6

0707
Art Director: Marcie Carson
Designers: Amy Klass, Cya Nelson
Client: U.S.C. Libraries
Software/Hardware: Mac, Adobe Illustrator,
Quark XPress, Adobe Photoshop

0709
Art Director: Marcie Carson
Designer: Cya Nelson
Client: U.S.C. School of Cinema & T.V.
Software/Hardware: Mac, Adobe Illustrator,
Adobe Photoshop, Quark XPress
Paper/Materials: Silver, Black & Varnish,
2-Color Foil Stamp

0918
Art Director: Marcie Carson
Designer: Amy Klass
Client: IE Design
Software/Hardware: Mac, Quark Xpress, Adobe
Illustrator, Adobe PhotoShop
Paper/Materials: Hanes T, 3 color

Image/Visual Communications
0392
Art Director: Dominick Sarica
Designer: Priska Diaz
Client: New York City College of Technology
Software/Hardware: Mac, Quark XPress,
Adobe Photoshop
Paper/Materials: Mohawk Superfine, 65 lb.
Ultra White Smooth

Image Zoo
0990
Art Director: Jamie Flint
Designer: Jamie Flint
Client: Arts Council NI
Software/Hardware: Mac, Adobe Photoshop
Paper/Materials: Helo Silk 210 gsm

Indian Hill Press
0013, 0125, 0128, 0142, 0145, 0148, 0166, 0167,
0168, 0204, 0214, 0215, 0216, 0257, 0268, 0271,
0274, 0318, 0319, 0321, 0322, 0324, 0335, 0336,
0393
Designer: Daniel A. Waters
Client: Indian Hill Press
Software/Hardware: Letterpress
Paper/Materials: Strathmore Pastelle

iNK design
0961
Designers: Wing Ngan, Maggie Cheung
Client: AIGA Boston
Printer: Postcardpress.com

Innova Ideas & Services
0575
Art Directors: Dawn Budd, Linda Griffen
Designer: Jessica Oakland
Client: Rachel Oakland
Software/Hardware: Quark Xpress

INOX Design
0860
Art Director: Creative Team
Designer: Masa Magnoni
Client: Italo & Tecla
Software/Hardware: Adobe Illustrator
Paper/Materials: Paper, Magnet

inpraxis, raum fur gestaitung
0471
Art Directors: A. Kranz & C. Schaffner
Designer: A. Kranz & C. Schaffner
Client: affetti strumentali
Software/Hardware: Quark XPress 4.01, Mac G4
Paper/Materials: 3 Color Offset printing on
240g Coated Stock

0788
Art Directors: A. Kranz & C. Schaffner
Designers: A. Kranz & C. Schaffner
Client: Objektform
Software/Hardware: Quark XPress 4.01, Mac G4
Paper/Materials: 5 Color Offset Printing on
240g Coated Stock

0800
Art Directors: A. Kranz, C. Schaffner
Designers: A. Kranz, C. Schaffner
Client: affetti strumentali
Software/Hardware: Quark XPress 4.0, Mac G4
Paper/Materials: Laser Coy on Different papers

Insight Design Communications
0505
Art Director: Tracy Holdeman
Designer: Lea Carmichael
Client: Jockeys & Juleps
Software/Hardware: Macromedia Freehand, Mac
Paper/Materials: Cougar Opaque White

0661
Art Director: Tracy Holdeman
Designer: Lea Carmichael
Client: Propaganda 101
Software/Hardware: Adobe Photoshop, Mac
Paper/Materials: Newsprint

0705
Art Director: Tracy Holdeman
Designer: Lea Carmichael
Client: Star Chefs
Software/Hardware: Adobe Photoshop, Mac
Paper/Materials: Cougar Opaque White

j

Jennifer Eaton Alden
0176
Client: Jennifer Eaton Alden

Jennifer Juliano Art, Design
0821
Art Director: Jennifer Juliano
Designer: Jennifer Juliano
Client: Jennifer Juliano
Software/Hardware: Mac, Adobe Illustrator
Paper/Materials: Somerset Velvet in Radiant
White & Neenah Classic Linen in Avon Brilliant
White

Jingleheimer Schmidt
0063, 0064, 0065, 0066, 0127, 0293, 0294, 0295,
0296, 0297, 0298, 0299, 0300, 0301, 0349, 0434,
0437, 0678
Art Director: Lane Foard
Designer: Lane Foard
Client: Squibnocket
Software/Hardware: Mac OS10/Quark Xpress

Jiva Creative
0745
Designer: Eric Lee
Client: Self
Software/Hardware: Quark XPress, Mac
Paper/Materials: Special Die Cut, Hand
Assembled Foil Stamp

Joao Machado Design Lda
0022
Art Director: Joao Machado
Designer: Joao Machado
Client: Almada's City Hall
Software/Hardware: Macromedia Freehand,
Quark XPress
Paper/Materials: Couche Mate

John Cameron
0354, 0355, 0356,
Paper/Materials: Wood Engravings Printed
Letterpress on Hahnemuhle Paper

John Evans Design
0052, 0114, 0087, 0098, 0149, 0198, 0199, 0316,
0367
Art Director: John Evans
Designer: John Evans
Client: Retail
Software/Hardware: Adobe Illustrator
Paper/Materials: 100# Porcelain Dull Cover

John Kallio Graphic Design
0261
Art Director: John Kallio
Client: John Kallio
Software/Hardware: Adobe Photoshop 5.5,
Quark XPress 3.3
Paper/Materials: Inkjet Printer

John Kneapler Design
0203
Art Director: John Kneapler
Designer: John Kneapler
Client: The Museum of Modern Art
Software/Hardware: Quark XPress
Paper/Materials: Coated Metallic

0306
Art Director: John Kneapler
Designers: Holly Buckley, John Kneapler
Client: MDMA
Software/Hardware: Adobe Illustrator
Paper/Materials: Coated Metallic

0406
Art Directors: Colleen Sheq, John Kneapler
Designer: Colleen Shea
Client: The Museum of Modern Art
Software/Hardware: Quark XPress
Paper/Materials: Coated White Foil Paper,
Few Stars

0585
Art Directors: Colleen Shea, John Kneapler
Designer: Colleen Shea,
Client: Hackensack University Medical Center
Paper/Materials: Velvet Peach Board &
Monadnock Dulcet

0644
Art Directors: Niccole White, John Kneapler
Designer: Niccole White
Client: The James Beard Foundation
Software/Hardware: Quark XPress
Paper/Materials: Monadnock Dulcet

0780
Art Directors: Colleen Shea, John Kneapler
Designer: Colleen Shea
Client: Hackensack University Medical Center
Software/Hardware: Adobe Illustrator 9.0
Paper/Materials: Covered White LOE Paper

Juicy Temples Creative
0587
Art Director: Klaus Heesch
Designers: Klaus Heesch, Mike Fusco,
Client: Juicy Temples Creative
Software/Hardware: Adobe Photoshop, Adobe
Illustrator, Mac
Paper/Materials: Brush, Paint, French
Parchtone White 65 lb. Cover, Vellum
Envelope

0820
Art Director: Klaus Heesch
Designers: Klaus Heesch, Mike Fusco
Client: Josh & January LeClair
Software/Hardware: Adobe Photoshop, Adobe
Illustrator, Mac

0857
Art Director: Klaus Heesch
Designer: Klaus Heesch
Client: Gregg & Adrian Hale
Software/Hardware: Typewriter, Photo Copier,
Pen, Adobe Photoshop, Adobe Illustrator, Mac
OS
Paper/Materials: Hand-printed on French
Smart White 130lb Cover, Vellum Envelope

Julia Tam Design
0070
Art Director: Julia Chong Tam
Designer: Julia Chong Tam
Client: Julia Tam Design
Software/Hardware: Adobe Illustrator, Quark
XPress
Paper/Materials: Coated Paper

Julie Vail Maw
0630
Art Director: Julie Vail Maw
Client: Wayne & Kelly Maw

0713
Art Director: Julie Vail Maw
Client: Jen & Rob Markowski

k

KBDA
0104, 0458, 0947
Art Director: Kim Baer
Designer: Jamie Diersing
Client: KBDA
Software/Hardware: Mac

0554
Art Director: Kim Baer
Designer: Keith Kneuven, Ramon Leander
Client: Shops on Lake Avenue
Software/Hardware: Mac

0889
Art Director: Kim Baer
Designer: Liz Burrill
Client: KBDA
Software/Hardware: Mac
Title: When Time Flies

Kehoe & Kehoe Design Associates
0303
Designer: Deborah Kehoe
Client: Kehoe & Kehoe Design Associates

0371
Art Director: Deborah Kehoe
Designer: Deborah Kehoe
Client: Kehoe & Kehoe Design Associates

0409
Designer: Deborah Kehoe
Client: Caroline Crawford

0808
Art Director: Deborah Kehoe
Designer: Lori Myers
Client: Kehoe & Kehoe Design Associates

Kendall Ross
0227
Art Director: David Kendall
Designers: Scott Fricsen, Helen Kong
Client: Kendall Ross
Software/Hardware: Adobe Illustrator, Mac
Paper/Materials: Vintage Velvet 80#C

0490
Art Director: David Kendall
Designer: David Kendall
Client: Bellevue Art Museum
Software/Hardware: Adobe Illustrator
Paper/Materials: Various

0508
Art Director: David Kendall
Designer: Shannon Ecke
Client: Tacoma Art Museum
Software/Hardware: Adobe Illustrator
Paper/Materials: Topkote 80#C

0793
Art Director: David Kendall
Designer: Josh Michas
Client: Tacoma Art Museum
Software/Hardware: Adobe Illustrator
Paper/Materials: Topkote

0992
Art Director: David Kendall
Designer: David Kendall
Client: Tacoma Art Museum
Software/Hardware: Adobe Illustrator
Paper/Materials: Topkote

Kevin Akers Design & Imagery
0350, 0416, 0436
Art Director: Kevin Akers
Designer: Kevin Akers
Client: Kevin & Judee Akers
Software/Hardware: Adobe Illustrator

0415
Art Director: Kevin Akers
Client: Kevin Akers Design & Imagery

0507, 0538, 0759
Art Director: Kevin Akers
Designer: Kevin Akers
Client: Philharmonic Baroque Orchestra

0942
Art Director: Kevin Akers
Client: Burson-Marsteller

0951
Art Director: Kevin Akers
Designer: Various
Client: Performance Printing

Kinetik
0962
Designers: Beth Clawson, Jeff Fabian,
Beverley Hunter, Mike Joosse, Katie Kroener,
Jackie Ratsch, Scott Rier, Sam Shelton, Jenny
Skillman
Client: Mark Finkenstaedt
Software/Hardware: Quark XPress, Mac

0974
Art Directors: Beth Clawson, Jeff Fabian,
Beverley Hunter, Mike Joosse, Katie Kroener,
Jackie Ratsch, Scott Rier, Sam Shelton,
Jenny Skillman
Designers: Beth Clawson, Jeff Fabian,
Beverley Hunter, Mike Joosse, Katie Kroener,
Jackie Ratsch, Scott Rier, Sam Shelton,
Jenny Skillman
Client: Kinetik
Software/Hardware: Quark XPress, Mac

KKargl Graphic Design
0473
Designer: Kathleen W. Kargl
Client: University of Dayton Alumni House
Software/Hardware: Macromedia Freehand

0682, 0796
Designer: Kathleen W. Kargl
Client: University of Dayton Rike Center Gallery
Software/Hardware: Macromedia Freehand

KO création
0194
Art Director: KO création
Designers: Pol Baril, Annie Lachapelle
Client: Bonaldo
Software/Hardware: Adobe InDesign
Paper/Materials: Horizon Silk cover 100lbs

0459
Art Director: KO création
Designer: Maxime Levesque
Client: IDX
Software/Hardware: Adobe Illustrator, Adobe
Photoshop
Paper/Materials: Tango 24 pts, Matte lamina-
tion

0616
Art Director: KO création
Designer: Christian Belanger
Client: Chants Libres
Software/Hardware: Adobe Illustrator, Adobe
Photoshop
Paper/Materials: Domtar Luna Cover 100 lbs.

0801
Art Director: Dennis Dulude
Designer: Dennis Dulude
Client: Marie Beaulieu & Mario Thibodeau
Software/Hardware: Adobe Illustrator
Paper/Materials: Domtar Solutions Cover
80lbs, Domtar Solutions Text 24lbs

0971
Art Director: Annie Lachapelle
Designer: Annie Lachapelle
Client: Christian Guay Photographe
Software/Hardware: Adobe InDesign, HB
Pencil, Right Hand
Paper/Materials: Horizon Silk Cover 100 lbs.

Knezic/Pavone
0435
Art Director: Robinson C. Smith
Designer: Robinson C. Smith
Client: Personal
Software/Hardware: Adobe Illustrator, Mac

Kolegram Design
0136
Art Director: Mike Teixeira
Designer: Andre Mitchell
Client: Kolegram Design
Software/Hardware: Quark XPress 4.0

0163
Art Director: Mike Teixeira
Designer: Jean-Francois Plante
Client: Kolegram Design
Software/Hardware: Quark XPress 4.0

0501
Art Director: Mike Teixeira
Designer: Annie Tanguay
Client: Tourisme-Outaouais
Software/Hardware: Quark XPress 4.0

0574
Art Director: Mike Teixeira
Designer: Mike Teixeira
Client: Advertising & Design Association
Software/Hardware: Quark XPress 4.0

0611
Art Director: Mike Teixeira
Designers: Annie Tanguay, Gontran Blais
Client: Kolegram Design
Software/Hardware: Quark XPress 4.0

0631
Art Director: Mike Teixeira
Designer: Jean-Francois Plante
Client: Portrait Gallery of Canada
Software/Hardware: Quark XPress 4.0

0684
Art Director: Mike Teixeira
Designer: Gontran Blais
Client: Buntin Reid Papers
Software/Hardware: Quark XPress 4.0

0915
Art Director: Mike Teixeira
Designer: Mike Teixeira
Client: Kolegram & Headlight Imagery
Software/Hardware: Quark XPress 4.0

0946
Art Director: Mike Teixeira
Designer: Mike Teixeira
Client: Kolegram Design
Software/Hardware: Quark XPress 4.0

Kristina E. Kim
0262, 0263, 0264, 0279, 0286, 0311, 0312, 0313
Client: Self-Promotion
Paper/Materials: Handmade Circle, Square
Punches, Scallop Scissors, Fox River Crushed
Leaf poppy Sparkles, 110 lb Cover Plus
Curious paper Metallics, Ice Gold, 93 lb.
Cover, Curious paper Metallics, Gold Leaf 92
lb. Cover, 3M Foam Tape

Kristin Cullen
0111, 0474
Designer: Kristin Cullen
Software/Hardware: Adobe Illustrator, Mac
Paper/Materials: French Frostone

0743
Designer: Kristin Cullen
Client: Kelly Ann & Kevin Flynn
Software/Hardware: Quark XPress, Adobe
Illustrator, Adobe Photoshop, Mac
Paper/Materials: French Frostone, Glama
Natural Vellum

Kristi Norgaard
0539
Client: Norgaard & Terleph

I

Laura McFadden Design, Inc.
0003
Art Director: Laura McFadden Design, Inc.
Designer: Laura McFadden Design, Inc.
Client: Laura McFadden
Software/Hardware: Quark XPress, Adobe
Photoshop
Paper/Materials: Paper

Laura Ploszaj
0861
Client: Sara Ploszaj
Software/Hardware: Quark XPress, Adobe
Illustrator
Paper/Materials: Strathmore Writing, Soft Blue
Cover, Letterpress

Leibow Studios
0540
Art Director: Paul Leibow
Designer: Paul Leibow
Client: Polo Gallery
Software/Hardware: Adobe Photoshop, Quark
XPress
Paper/Materials: Coated Card Stock

0666
Art Director: Paul Leibow
Designer: Paul Leibow
Client: The Liquid Gallery
Software/Hardware: Adobe Photoshop, Quark
XPress
Paper/Materials: Coated Card Stock

0758
Art Director: Paul Leibow
Designer: Paul Leibow
Client: Parker Gallery
Software/Hardware: Adobe Photoshop, Quark
XPress
Paper/Materials: Coated Card Stock

0925
Art Director: Paul Leibow
Designer: Paul Leibow
Client: Leibow Studios
Software/Hardware: Adobe Photoshop, Quark
XPress
Paper/Materials: Coated Card Stock

Lemley Design Company
0895
Art Director: David Lemley
Designers: David Lemley, Yuri Shuets
Client: Lemley Design Company
Software/Hardware: Macromedia Freehand 10
Paper/Materials: White Cover Stock, Beef
Jerky, Vacuum Seal Wrap

0965
Art Director: David Lemley
Designers: David Lemley, Yuri Shuets
Client: Lemley Design Company
Software/Hardware: Macromedia Freehand 10,
Adobe Photoshop 6.0, Mac 64
Paper/Materials: Neenah Paper, Red Ribbon,
Silver Eyelets

Les Cheneaux Design
0044
Designer: Lori Young
Client: Les Cheneaux Design
Software/Hardware: Mac OS 9.5
Paper/Materials: Silver Painted Card Stock with
Affixed Card

0511
Designer: Lori Young
Client: Ashford Village Block Party
Software/Hardware: Quark XPress 3.3, Adobe
Illustrator 9.0
Paper/Materials: #70 Matte Card Stock

Letter Design
0934
Art Director: Paul Shaw
Designer: Paul Shaw
Client: Paul Shaw
Software/Hardware: Quark XPress, Mac
Paper/Materials: Strathmore Writing

Likovni Studio D.O.O.
0059, 0160
Client: Likovni Studio D.O.O.
Software/Hardware: Macromedia Freehand, Mac
Paper/Materials: Magnomatt

0496
Client: Archaeological Museum Zagreb
Software/Hardware: Macromedia Freehand, Mac
Paper/Materials: Magnomatt

Liquid Agency, Inc.
0610
Art Director: Lisa Kliman
Designer: Julia Held
Client: San Jose Downtown Association
Software/Hardware: Quark XPress, Mac

Little Smiles Co.
0097, 0186, 0736
Art Director: Stephanie Zelman
Client: Little Smiles Co.

Lloyds Graphic Design
0455
Art Director: Alexander Lloyd
Designer: Alexander Lloyd
Client: Alexander Lloyd
Software/Hardware: Mac, Macromedia
Freehand, Adobe Photoshop
Paper/Materials: Matt 300 gsm.

0621
Art Director: Alexander Lloyd
Designer: Alexander Lloyd
Client: Marlborough District Council
Software/Hardware: Mac, Macromedia
Freehand
Paper/Materials: Gloss Art 150 gms

0728
Art Director: Alexander Lloyd
Designer: Alexander Lloyd
Client: Bay of Many Coves Resort
Software/Hardware: Mac, Macromedia
Freehand
Paper/Materials: Matt Art 300 gsm

0924
Art Director: Alexander Lloyd
Designer: Alexander Lloyd
Client: Accord Insurance
Software/Hardware: Mac, Macromedia
Freehand, Adobe Photoshop
Paper/Materials: Coated Card Stock

Logica3 Ltd
0039
Art Director: Lisa Page
Designer: Phil Oster
Client: Big Leap Media
Software/Hardware: Quark XPress, Mac
Paper/Materials: Mohawk Superfine, 100#
Cover

Loudmouth Graphics
0466
Art Director: David Schroer
Designer: David Schroer
Client: David Schroer, Sue Mullins
Software/Hardware: Mac, Quark XPress,
Adobe Photoshop
Paper/Materials: 80# McCoy Velour Cover,
Gloss UV Coating

Louey/Rubino Design Group
0953
Art Director: Robert Louey
Designers: Robert Louey, Javier Leguizamo
Client: Louey/Rubino Design Group
Software/Hardware: Quark XPress
Paper/Materials: Fox River Paper

Love Communication
0613
Art Director: Preston Wood
Designer: Craig Lee
Client: Novell Utah Showdown
Software/Hardware: Adobe Photoshop, Adobe
Illustrator, Quark XPress
Paper/Materials: 80lb Cover Lustro

0650
Art Director: Preston Wood
Designer: Preston Wood
Client: Love Communication
Software/Hardware: Adobe Photoshop, Quark
XPress, Adobe Illustrator
Paper/Materials: Pain Can, Confetti, Lustro
Dull

0875
Art Director: Preston Wood
Designer: Craig Lee
Client: Green Space Design
Software/Hardware: Adobe Photoshop, Quark
XPress, Adobe Illustrator
Paper/Materials: French Cordform

m

MA & Associados
0102
Art Director: Mario Aurelio
Designer: Mario Aurelio
Client: MCI
Software/Hardware: Mac, Macromedia Freehand
Paper/Materials: Couchet

0494
Art Director: Mario Aurelio
Designer: Mario Aurelio
Client: Fuel
Software/Hardware: Mac, Macromedia Freehand
Paper/Materials: Couchet Mate

0512
Art Director: Mario Aurelio
Designer: Mario Aurelio
Client: Onara
Software/Hardware: Mac, Macromedia Freehand
Paper/Materials: Couchet

0543
Art Director: Mario Aurelio
Designer: Mario Aurelio
Client: Inovacao
Software/Hardware: Mac, Macromedia Freehand
Paper/Materials: Couchet Mate

0635
Art Director: Mario Aurelio
Designer: Mario Aurelio
Client: MCI
Software/Hardware: Mac, Macromedia Freehand
Paper/Materials: Couchet Mate

0636
Art Director: Mario Aurelio
Designer: Mario Aurelio
Client: Fuel
Software/Hardware: Mac, Macromedia Freehand
Paper/Materials: Ikonofix

0646
Art Director: Mario Aurelio
Designer: Mario Aurelio
Client: Onara
Software/Hardware: Mac, Macromedia Freehand
Paper/Materials: Star Dream

0830
Art Director: Mario Aurelio
Designer: Mario Aurelio
Client: Fuel
Software/Hardware: Mac, Macromedia Freehand
Paper/Materials: Star Dream

M-Art
0561
Art Director: Marty Ittner
Designer: Marty Ittner
Client: Rae Rosenthal
Software/Hardware: Quark XPress,
Macromedia Freehand
Paper/Materials: Classic Columns, Screenprint
& Silver Seal

0855
Art Director: Marty Ittner
Designer: Marty Ittner
Client: National Osteoporosis Foundation
Software/Hardware: Quark XPress,
Macromedia Freehand
Paper/Materials: Strathmore Elements,
Gilclear, Fraser Passport

Maren Bottger
0432
Client: Family of Designer
Software/Hardware: Macromedia Freehand,
Adobe Photoshop, Mac OS
Paper/Materials: Laser Print on Card

0859
Client: Family of Designer
Software/Hardware: Macromedia Freehand,
Mac OS
Paper/Materials: Various Paper & Card, Round
Metal Paperclips

Marlena Sang
0834
Client: Friends
Software/Hardware: Quark XPress
Paper/Materials: Munken Pure 240gm3,
Envelope, Cromatico Zinnober

Martin Lemelman Illustration
0400
Art Director: Martin Lemelman
Client: Martin Lemelman
Software/Hardware: Mac, Adobe Illustrator

Marty Blake Graphic Design
0452
Art Director: Marty Blake
Designer: Marty Blake
Client: Parmigiano Reggiano, U.S. Office
Software/Hardware: Mac, Adobe Illustrator,
Fotographer
Paper/Materials: Fox River, Sundance, Confetti

0669
Art Director: Marty Blake
Designer: Marty Blake
Client: Everson Museum of Art
Software/Hardware: Mac, Adobe Photoshop,
Quark XPress
Paper/Materials: Silk- Job Parilux

Matsumoto Incorporated
0060
Art Director: Takaaki Matsumoto
Designer: Takaaki Matsumoto
Client: Matsumoto Incorporated
Software/Hardware: Quark XPress
Paper/Materials: Letterpress, Somerset White
Velvet, 300 gm

0376
Art Director: Takaaki Matsumoto
Designer: Takaaki Matsumoto
Client: Matsumoto Incorporated
Software/Hardware: Quark XPress
Paper/Materials: Offset printing with Metallic
Inks, Neenah Classic Cream 130lb Cover

McCullough Creative Group, Inc.
0209
Designer: McCullough Creative Team
Client: McCullough Creative Group
Software/Hardware: Adobe Photoshop,
Macromedia Freehand, Mac
Paper/Materials: Ribbon, Tinsel, Ornament
Hooks

0248
Designer: Greg Dietzenbach
Client: McCullough Creative Group
Software/Hardware: Macromedia Freehand, Mac
Paper/Materials: Wire Spiral-Bound

0524
Designer: Erin Germain
Client: Dubuque Bank & Trust
Software/Hardware: Quark/Mac
Paper/Materials: Copper grommet binding,
Wausau Royal Fiber paperstock

0537
Designer: Roger Scholbrock
Client: John Deere Construction & Forestry
Company
Software/Hardware: Adobe Photoshop,
Macromedia Freehand, Mac
Paper/Materials: Wooden Dowel, Rubber Band

McGINTY

0273
Art Director: Matt Rue
Designers: Matt Rue, Kyle Russell
Software/Hardware: Adobe Photoshop

Megan Cooney

0072
Client: Megan Cooney

0579
Client: Megan Cooney

Megan Webber Design

0138
Designers: Megan Webber, Wendy Carnegie
Client: Megan Webber
Software/Hardware: Adobe Illustrator
Paper/Materials: Verigood Blotting, Letterpress
Printing

0185
Designer: Megan Webber
Client: Megan Webber Design
Software/Hardware: Adobe Illustrator
Paper/Materials: 1-Color Silk-Screen on
Carnival White 65#C

0366
Designers: Megan Webber, Wendy Carnegie,
Julie Savakis
Client: Megan Webber
Software/Hardware: Adobe Illustrator
Paper/Materials: Vertigos Blotting, 2-Color
Letterpress

Metzler & Associes

0153
Art Director: M. A. Herrmann
Designer: A. Pavion
Client: Metzler & Associes
Software/Hardware: Adobe Illustrator,
Macromedia Flash MX

0278
Art Director: M.A. Herrmann
Designer: A. Martirene
Client: Metzler & Associes
Software/Hardware: Adobe Illustrator, Mac

Michael Courtney Design

0488
Art Director: Michael Courtney
Designer: Michael Courtney
Client: Christine O'Leary
Software/Hardware: Macromedia Freehand

0535
Art Director: Michael Courtney
Designers: Heidi Fanour, Michael Courtney,
Margaret Longi
Client: Bellevue Arts Commission
Software/Hardware: Macromedia Freehand,
Adobe Photoshop

0548
Art Director: Michael Courtney
Designers: Micahel Courtney, Debra Burgess
Client: Tops Art Fest
Software/Hardware: Macromedia Freehand,
Adobe Photoshop
Paper/Materials: Cut Paper, Pastel, Marker

0921
Art Director: Michael Courtney
Designers: Michael Courtney, Karen Cramer,
Heidi Favour, Margaret Long, Jennifer Comer,
Lauren DiRusso
Client: Michael Courtney Design
Software/Hardware: Macromedia Freehand,
Adobe Photoshop
Paper/Materials: Embossed Paper, Copper Tag
(Etched), 4/C Offset on Uncoated Stock,
Vellum

Michael Osborne Design

0075
Art Director: Michael Osborne
Client: Michael Osborne Design
Software/Hardware: Adobe Illustrator, Mac
Paper/Materials: Summerset

0110
Art Director: Michael Osborne
Designer: Michelle Regenbogen
Client: Michael Osborne Design
Software/Hardware: Adobe Illustrator, Mac
Paper/Materials: Summerset

0277
Art Director: Michael Osborne
Designers: Paul Kagiwada/Michelle Regen
Bogen
Client: Michael Osborne Design
Software/Hardware: Adobe Illustrator, Mac
Paper/Materials: Strathmore

0353
Art Director: Michael Osborne
Client: Michael Osborne Design
Software/Hardware: Adobe Illustrator, Mac
Paper/Materials: Cranes

0933
Art Director: Michael Osborne
Designer: Michelle Regenbogen
Client: Fox River Paper
Software/Hardware: Adobe Illustrator, Mac
Paper/Materials: Starwhite

Mike Quon/Designation

0746
Art Director: Mike Quon
Designer: Mike Quon
Client: Mike Quon/Tulsa ADC
Software/Hardware: Adobe Illustrator, Mac
Paper/Materials: Cover Stock

Milk Row Studio/Press

0091
Art Director: Keith D. Cross
Designer: Keith D. Cross
Client: (self-promotional greeting)
Paper/Materials: Metal, Ink, Paper, Press,
Hand Set Type & Ornamenes Printed
Letterpress on Neenah Solar White 110 lb.
Cover

0649
Art Director: Keith D. Cross
Designer: Keith D. Cross
Client: The Letterpress Guild of New England
Paper/Materials: Metal, Ink, Paper, Press,
Handset Type, Ornaments Printed Letterpress
on Neenah, Classic Crest, Ember Blue 80lb.
Cover

0807
Art Director: Keith D. Cross
Designer: Keith D. Cross
Client: Peter Pinch & Catherine Yu
Software/Hardware: Metal, Ink, Paper, Press
Paper/Materials: Linocut Illustrations, Handset
Type, Neenah Saw Grass, 80lb. Cover

0818
Art Director: Keith D. Cross
Designer: Keith D. Cross
Client: Allen Hiltz & Erin McGee
Software/Hardware: Adobe Photoshop 6.0,
Macromedia Freehand 9.0
Paper/Materials: Metal, Ink, Paper, Press,
Handset Type & Illustration Printed from Plate,
Gilbert Voice Slate & Chalk

Mindwalk Design Group, Inc.

0232
Art Director: Michael Huggins
Client: Mindwalk Design Group
Software/Hardware: Adobe Illustrator, Quark
Express, Mac

Miro Design

0028, 0029, 0049, 0121, 0156, 0159, 0162, 0266
Designer: Judy Glenzer
Client: Aardvark Letterpress/Syndicate Design
Software/Hardware: Adobe Illustrator
Paper/Materials: Lana Watercolor Paper

Mirage Design

0308, 0328
Art Director: Mark LaPointe
Designer: Lynette Allaire
Client: Mirage Design
Software/Hardware: Macromedia Freehand, Mac

0763
Art Director: Mark LaPointe
Designer: Lynette Allaire
Client: Boston Municipal Research Bureau
Software/Hardware: Macromedia Freehand, Mac

0852
Art Director: Mark LaPointe
Designer: Lynette Allaire
Client: Massachusetts High Technology
Council
Software/Hardware: Macromedia Freehand, Mac

Mirko Ilic Corp

0454
Art Director: Mirko Ilic
Designers: Mirko Ilic, Heath Hingardner
Client: Levy Creative

0586
Art Director: Mirko Ilic
Designers: Mirko Ilic, Heath Hindgardner
Client: Auschwitz Jewish Center

0911
Art Director: Mirko Ilic
Designer: Mirko Ilic
Client: K-Space

Misha Design Studio

0025
Art Director: Misha Lenn
Designer: Misha Lenn
Client: City of Boston
Software/Hardware: Watercolor

0061
Art Director: Misha Lenn
Designer: Misha Lenn
Client: Boston Symphony Orchestra
Paper/Materials: Watercolor

0108
Art Director: Misha Lenn
Designer: Misha Lenn
Client: Filene's Basement
Paper/Materials: Naturoles

M. J. Bronstein
0320
Art Director: M. J. Bronstein
Designer: M. J. Bronstein
Client: M. J. Bronstéin
Software/Hardware: Adobe Photoshop, Mac OS
Paper/Materials: Ultra Premium Brilliant White
Card Stock with Aqueous Coating

Momentum Press and Design
0907
Art Director: Jill Vartenigian
Designer: Jill Vartenigian
Client: Kathleen Kenneally Acupuncture
Paper/Materials: Wood Type, Lead Type, Rives
BFK, Letterpress Printed On a 10X15 C & P

Muse Inspired
0033, 0034, 0035, 0347, 0352
Art Director: Victoria Kens
Designer: Victoria Kens
Client: Muse Inspired

Muzak Marketing
0739
Art Director: Bob Finigan
Designer: David Eller
Client: Muzak
Software/Hardware: Macromedia Freehand 10,
Mac
Paper Materials: Self-Sealing Poly Envelope,
Fasson Fastrack Pressure Sensitive Label,
60 lb. Recycled Lynx Opaque Smooth Finish

0891
Art Director: Bob Finigan
Designer: David Eller
Client: Muzak
Software/Hardware: Macromedia Freehand 10,
Mac
Paper/Materials: Inserts – Mohawk Options
TrueWhite, 96 Smooth 130 dic; Envelope –
Mohawk Options TrueWhite, 96 Vellum 130
dic

0894
Art Director: Bob Finigan
Designer: David Eller
Client: Muzak and Karim Rashid, Inc.
Software/Hardware: Macromedia Freehand 10,
Mac
Paper/Materials: 60 lb. Recycled Lynx Opaque
Smooth Finish

0996
Designer: David Eller
Client: Muzak & Karim Rashid, Inc.
Software/Hardware: Macromedia Freehand 10,
Mac
Paper/Materials: Laminated Film Pouch, Heat-
Sealed, 100lb Starwhite Mohawk,
Superfine Cover, Ultra White

n

Nassar Design
0078
Art Director: Nelida Nassar
Designers: Margarita Encomienda, Nelida
Nassar
Client: Nassar Design
Software/Hardware: Quark XPress
Paper/Materials: Gross Grain Ribbon & #100
Text Onancock Dulcet Smooth

0120
Art Director: Nelida Nassar
Designers: Margarita Encomienda, Nelida
Nassar
Client: Nassar Design
Software/Hardware: Quark XPress, Adobe
Photoshop
Paper/Materials: #30 Text Chartham
Translucents Platinum, #27 Chromatic Flue
Pink
Envelope #27 Chromatic Mango

0205
Art Director: Nelida Nassar
Designers: Margarita Encomienda, Nelida
Nassar
Client: Hybrid
Software/Hardware: Quark XPress, Adobe
Illustrator
Paper/Materials:12pt One-Side Cover
Kromekote Glass

0233
Art Director: Nelida Nassar
Designers: Margarita Encomienda, Nelida
Nassar
Client: Weidlinger Associates, Inc.
Software/Hardware: Quark XPress, Adobe
Photoshop, Adobe Illustrator
Paper/Materials: #92 Cover Arjo Wiggins
Keaykolour Metallics Anodized
Envelope #20 Chartham Translucents Ocean
Blue

0246
Art Director: Nelida Nassar
Designers: Margarita Encomienda, Nelida
Nassar
Client: Sea-Dar Enterprises
Software/Hardware: Quark XPress, Adobe
Illustrator
Paper/Materials: #100 cover Mohawk
Superfine Ultrawhite Smooth

0309
Art Director: Nelida Nassar
Designers: Margarita Encomienda, Nelida
Nassar
Client: Nassar Design
Software/Hardware: Quark XPress
Paper/Materials: Mylar Cracked Ice Burgundy

0407
Art Director: Nelida Nassar
Designers: Margarita Encomienda, Nelida
Nassar
Client: The Stubbins Associates, Inc.
Software/Hardware: Quark XPress, Adobe
Illustrator
Paper/Materials: #53 Cover Arjo Wiggins
Curious Translucent Gold Iridescent

0440
Art Director: Nelida Nassar
Designers: Margarita Encomienda, Nelida
Nassar
Client: Weidlinger Associates, Inc.
Software/Hardware: Quark XPress, Adobe
Photoshop
Paper/Materials: #100 Cover Mohawk
Superfine White plus Matching Envelopes

0461
Art Director: Nelida Nassar
Designers: Margarita Encomienda, Nelida
Nassar
Client: The Stubbins Associates, Inc.
Software/Hardware: Quark XPress, Adobe
Illustrator
Paper/Materials: #80 Cover Sappi Strobe Silk

0605
Art Director: Nelida Nassar
Designers: Margarita Encomienda, Nelida
Nassar
Client: Artisans du Liban et d'Orient
Software/Hardware: Quark XPress, Adobe
Illustrator
Paper/Materials: #92.5 Cover Zanders Ikono
Dull Satin

0670
Art Director: Nelida Nassar
Designers: Margarita Encomienda, Nelida
Nassar
Client: Harvard Design School
Software/Hardware: Quark XPress, Adobe
Illustrator
Paper/Materials: #100 Cover Sappi Vintage
Gloss

0835
Art Director: Nelida Nassar
Designers: Margarita Encomienda, Nelida
Nassar
Client: Harvard Design School
Software/Hardware: Quark XPress, Adobe
Photoshop
Paper/Materials: #100 Mohawk Superfine
Ultrawhite Smooth Double-Thick

0880
Art Director: Nelida Nassar
Designers: Margarita Encomienda, Nelida
Nassar
Client: Weidlinger Associates, Inc.
Software/Hardware: Quark XPress, Adobe
Photoshop, Adobe Illustrator
Paper/Materials: #92 Cover Arjo Wiggins
Keaykolour Metallics Galvanised

0906
Art Director: Nelida Nassar
Designers: Margarita Encomienda, Nelida
Nassar
Client: Jacques Liger-Belair
Software/Hardware: Quark XPress, Adobe
Illustrator
Paper/Materials: #92.5 Cover Zanders
Ikono Matt

0943
Art Director: Nelida Nassar
Designers: Margarita Encomienda, Nelida
Nassar
Client: Leers Weizapfel Architects Associates, Inc.
Software/Hardware: Quark Xpress, Adobe
Illustrator
Paper/Materials: #80 Cover Sappi Vintage
Velvet

0998
Art Director: Nelida Nassar
Designers: Margarita Encomienda, Nelida Nassar
Client: The Stubbins Associates, Inc.
Software/Hardware: Quark XPress, Adobe Photoshop
Paper/Materials: #80 Cover Sappi Strobe Silk

New Idea Design
0541
Designer: Ron Boldt
Client: Regional West Medical Center
Software/Hardware: Macromedia Freehand 7.0, Mac

Nexus
0360
Art Director: Arvi Raquel-Santos
Designer: Avvi Raquel-Santos
Client: Self-Promotion Christmas Card
Software/Hardware: Adobe Illustrator, Mac
Paper/Materials: Colored Pencil (Hand Colored)

Nickelodeon Creative Resources
0500
Art Director: Theresa Fitzgerald
Designer: Erin Blankley
Client: Klasky-Csupo
Software/Hardware: Adobe Illustrator
Paper/Materials: Semigloss Cardstock, Z Metallic Inks, Star Confetti

Nielinger & Rohsiepe
0202
Photographer: Christian Nielinger
Designer: Herbert Rohsiepe
Client: Christian Nielinger & Herbert Rohsiepe
Software/Hardware: Macromedia Freehand, Mac
Paper/Materials: Arjo Wiggins Impressions

9SpotMonk Design Co.
0463
Art Director: Vivian Leung
Designer: Vivian Leung
Client: Jill & Paul Roebinson
Software/Hardware: Macromedia Freehand MX
Paper/Materials: Arches Paper, Cromatica Envelopes Printed via Letterpress

0477
Art Director: Vivian Leung
Designer: Vivian Leung
Client: Jill & Paul Roebinson
Software/Hardware: Macromedia Freehand MX
Paper/Materials: Arches Paper, Cromatica Envelopes

0565
Art Director: Vivian Leung
Designer: Vivian Leung
Client: Marjorie Slatin & Diego Vasquez
Software/Hardware: Mac, Macromedia Freehand MX
Paper/Materials: Pescia Paper, Custom Envelope, Printed Via Letterpress

0568
Art Director: Vivian Leung
Designer: Vivian Leung
Client: Vivian Leung & Erik Naranjo
Software/Hardware: Mac, Macromedia Freehand MX
Paper/Materials: Somerset Cards, Arturo Envelopes, Printed via Letterpress

0570
Art Director: Vivian Leung
Designer: Vivian Leung
Client: Margrethe Jacobson & Collin McDermott
Software/Hardware: Mac, Macromedia Freehand MX
Paper/Materials: Somerset paper, Arturo Envelopes, Printed via Letterpress

0618
Art Director: Vivian Leung
Designer: Vivian Leung
Client: Catalina Grimaldi & Stephano DiAlessandro
Software/Hardware: Mac, Macromedia Freehand MX
Paper/Materials: Somerset Paper, Arturo Envelope, Printed via Letterpress

Noon
0446
Art Director: Cinthia Wen
Designer: Cinthia Wen
Client: Greg Shove
Software/Hardware: Adobe Photoshop, Adobe Illustrator, Mac

0910
Art Director: Cinthia Wen
Designer: Claudia Fung
Software/Hardware: Adobe Illustrator, Mac
Paper/Materials: Starwhite Vicksburg, Fresh Rosemary

0950
Art Director: Cinthia Wen
Designer: Cinthia Wen
Software/Hardware: Adobe Illustrator, Mac
Paper/Materials: Handmade Paper, Gmund Envelopes (GER)

O

OrangeSeed Design
0672
Art Director: Damien Wolf
Designers: Damien Wolf, Rebecca Miles
Client: Andersen Corporation
Software/Hardware: Adobe Photoshop, Quark XPress, Mac G4
Paper/Materials: Curious Papers, Anodized & Ice Gold 92lb Cover, Anodized A7 Envelopes

0972
Art Director: Damien Wolf
Designers: Damien Wolf, Phil Hoch
Client: OrangeSeed Design
Software/Hardware: Adobe Illustrator, Adobe Photoshop, Quark XPress, Mac G4
Paper/Materials: Wood Orange Crate & Anchor Paper-Proterra Straw 70lb Text

p

Palm Press
0009
Art Director: Theresa McCormac
Client: Retail Sales

Palo Alto Junior Museum & Zoo
0144
Designer: Efrat Rafaeli
Client: Palo Alto Junior Museum & Zoo
Software/Hardware: Adobe Illustrator
Paper/Materials: Carolina CISO

0778
Designer: Efrat Rafaeli
Client: Palo Alto Junior Museum & Zoo
Software/Hardware: Adobe Illustrator
Paper/Materials: Cougar

0797
Designer: Efrat Rafaeli
Client: Palo Alto Junior Museum & Zoo
Software/Hardware: Adobe Illustrator
Paper/Materials: Card Stock

Pangaro Beer
0007
Art Directors: Natalie Pangaro, Shannon Beer
Designers: Natalie Pangaro, Shannon Beer
Client: Pangaro Beer
Software/Hardware: Quark XPress 4.0
Paper/Materials: Strathmore-Ultimate White 80# Cover

0344
Art Directors: Natalie Pangard, Shannon Beer
Designers: David Salafia, Joanna DeFazio
Client: Pangard Beer
Software/Hardware: Quark XPress
Paper/Materials: Strathmore

0544
Art Directors: Natalie Pangard, Shannon Beer
Designer: David Salafia
Client: Harvard Medical School
Software/Hardware: Quark XPress 4.0
Paper/Materials: Gilbert Realm

0598
Art Directors: Natalie Pangard, Shannon Beer
Designer: David Salafia
Client: Harvard Medical School
Software/Hardware: Quark XPress 4.0
Paper/Materials: Gilbert Realm, Natural

0637
Art Directors: Natalie Pangard, Shannon Beer
Designer: David Salafia
Client: Mellon
Software/Hardware: Quark XPress 4.0

0762
Art Directors: Natalie Pangard, Shannon Beer
Designers: David Salafia, Joanna DeFazio
Client: The Art Institute of Boston
Software/Hardware: Quark XPress 4.0
Paper/Materials: Scheufelen, Phoendstarr 80# Cover Dull

Paper Lantern Press
0048
Art Director: Michelle Farinella
Designer: Michelle Farinella
Client: Paper Lantern Press
Software/Hardware: Mac, Quark XPress, Adobe Photoshop
Paper/Materials: Gilbert Realm

0147
Art Director: Michelle Farinella
Designers: Michelle Farinella, Judith Wolf
Client: Paper Lantern Press
Software/Hardware: Quark XPress, Mac, Adobe Photoshop
Paper/Materials: Gilbert Realm

0150
Art Director: Michelle Farinella
Designers: Michelle Farinella, Judith Wolf
Client: Paper Lantern Press
Software/Hardware: Mac, Quark XPress, Adobe Photoshop
Paper/Materials: Vintage Velvet

Partners in Print
0659
Art Director: Ariel Janzen
Designer: Ariel Janzen
Client: Laurel Crockett, Drew Rector
Software/Hardware: Adobe Illustrator
Paper/Materials: Vellum, Handmade Papers, Original Calligraphy

Paul Shaw Letter Design
0291
Designer: Paul Shaw
Client: Paul Shaw Letter Design & Peter Kruty Editions

Peggy Pelletier
0031, 0092, 0093, 0368, 0369
Paper/Materials: Handmade Swatchbook Scraps, Old Paper Promotions

Pernsteiner Creative Group, Inc.
0629
Art Director: Todd Pernsteiner
Designer: Andy Hauck
Client: County Concrete Corporation
Software/Hardware: Adobe Photoshop, Quark XPress, Mac
Paper/Materials: 125# Manilla Tag, 100# Mounte Matte Text

Peter Kruty Editions
0408
Designer: Alexander Ku
Client: Alexander Ku & Jane Yemzas Ku

0813
Designer: Sayre Gaydos
Client: Kristin Newman Designs

0847
Designer: Sayre Gaydos

plus design, inc.
0076
Art Director: Anita Meyer
Designer: Anita Meyer
Software/Hardware: Quark XPress, by Hand
Paper/Materials: Curious Paper Bronze Ore, Cover 92 lb, Tissue Paper, Ribbon, Silver Thread

0422
Art Directors: Anita Meyer, Karin Fickett, Dina Zaccagnini, Matthew Monk
Designers: Anita Meyer, Karin Fickett, Dina Zaccagnini, Matthew Monk, Jan Baker
Client: Plus Design, Inc.
Paper/Materials: Cloth, Silkscreener

0504
Art Director: Anita Meyer
Designers: Anita Meyer, Vivian Law
Client: Princeton University Art Museum
Software/Hardware: Quark XPress, Mac

0577
Art Director: Anita Meyer
Designer: Anita Meyer
Client: The Cloud Foundation
Software/Hardware: Quark XPress, Mac

0822
Art Director: Anita Meyer
Designers: Anita Meyer, Jan Baker
Client: plus design inc.
Software/Hardware: Letterpress
Paper/Materials: Handmade Paper-Made from Old Sheets, Cloth, Flowers, Hair & Books

0935
Art Directors: Anita Meyer, Karin Fickett
Designers: Anita Meyer, Vivian Law, Karin Fickett, Kristin Hughes
Client: Plus Design, Inc.
Software/Hardware: Quark Xpress, Mac
Paper/Materials: Recycled press sheets, static shielding bag, carpentry pencils
Title: New Year's Gift

Popcorn Initiative
0071
Art Directors: Chris Jones, Roger Wood
Designers: Chris Jones, Roger Wood
Client: Popcorn Initiative
Software/Hardware: Mac G4-500 Megahertz, 5" X 8" Kelsey, Excelsior LetterPress
Paper/Materials: French Paper, Frostone 140 lb. Cover, Glacier & Lots of Wire

0675
Art Directors: Chris Jones, Roger Wood
Designers: Chris Jones, Roger Wood
Client: Popcorn Initiative
Software/Hardware: Mac G4-500 Megahertz
Paper/Materials: Table Saw, Via Paper, White 100lb Text, Burlap & Grommets

Porto & Martinez Design Studio
0428
Art Directors: Bruno Porto, Marcelo Martinez
Designer: Bruno Porto
Client: Madina Artes Graficas
Software/Hardware: Quark XPress, Mac, Adobe Photoshop
Paper/Materials: 4-Color Die-Cut Popup

0831
Art Directors: Marcelo Martinez, Bruno Porto
Designer/Illustrator: Marcelo Martinez
Client: Marcelo Martinez, Renata Arlota
Software/Hardware: Quark XPress, Macromedia Freehand, Adobe Photoshop, Mac
Paper/Materials: Color Print on Elements, Soft White Dots 216g

Prank
0628
Client: Art Institute of Boston Class of '03
Paper/Materials: Silkscreen, Hanes Size 4 Boys

Pure Imagination Studios
0827
Art Director: Josh Williams
Designer: Josh Williams
Client: Rachel & Josh Williams
Software/Hardware: Penlink, Macromedia Freehand, Mac OS 10
Paper/Materials: Strathmore Writing Cover, Neenah Uv ultra II

r

R2 design
0625
Art Directors: Liza Defossez Ramalho, Artur Rebelo
Designers: Lize Defossez Ramalho & Artur Rebelo
Client: Marta & Gil
Software/Hardware: Macromedia Freehand 9.0
Paper/Materials: Recycled Cardboard, Bright Paper

0722
Art Directors: Liza Defossez Ramalho, Artur Rebelo
Designers: Liza Defossez Ramalho, Artur Rebelo
Client: Cassiopeia
Software/Hardware: Macromedia Freehand 9.0
Paper/Materials: Recycled Cardboard

Range
0521
Art Director: Steve Richard
Designer: Amy Becker-Jones
Client: Canton High School-Class of 1993 Reunion
Software/Hardware: Quark XPress, Adobe Photoshop, Mac
Paper/Materials: French Paper, Starch White, 120 lb Cover, Hand Silk Screened

0556
Art Director: Steve Richard
Client: Juvenile Diabetes Research Foundation-NH
Software/Hardware: Quark XPress, Adobe Photoshop
Paper/Materials: Domtar Feltweave

Red Design
0137
Art Director: Red Design
Designer: Red Design
Client: Red Design
Software/Hardware: Macromedia Freehand, Mac
Paper/Materials: Card

0411
Art Director: Red Design
Designer: Red Design
Client: Ourselves
Software/Hardware: Macromedia Freehand
Paper/Materials: Wood

Red Alert Design
0920
Art Directors: Jon Wainwright, Matt Sanerman
Designers: Jon Wainwright, Matt Sanderman
Client: Red Alert Design
Software/Hardware: Adobe Illustrator, Mac
Paper/Materials: Inflatable Plastic Bag, Screen Print

Refinery Design Company
0101, 0329, 0787
Art Director: Mike Schmalz
Designer: Julie Schmalz
Client: DHCU
Software/Hardware: Mac, Macromedia Freehand

0576
Art Director: Mike Schmalz
Designer: Julie Schmalz
Client: Joe & Trisha Hearn
Software/Hardware: Mac, Macromedia Freehand

0754
Art Director: Mike Schmalz
Designer: Julie Schmalz
Client: Rick & Kim Dehn
Software/Hardware: Mac, Micromedia
Freehand

0806
Art Director: Mike Schmalz
Designer: Mike Schmalz
Client: Mike & Julie Schmalz
Software/Hardware: Mac, Macromedia
Freehand

re.salzman designs
0854
Art Directors: Rick Salzman, Ida Cheinman
Designers: Rick Salzman, Ida Cheinman
Client: Adler Display
Software/Hardware: Mac, Adobe Illustrator 10
Paper/Materials: 120lb Cover, Dull Productolith

Rick Johnson & Company
0178
Art Director: Mark Chamblain
Designer: Tim McGrath
Client: United Blood Services
Software/Hardware: Quark XPress, Mac
Paper/Materials: Candy Box, White Candy
Cane

0619
Designer: Tim McGrath
Client: Los Alamos National Bank
Software/Hardware: Quark XPress, Adobe
Illustrator
Paper/Materials: Classic Crest

0858
Designer: Tim McGrath
Client: Los Alamos National Bank
Software/Hardware: Quark XPress, Adobe
Illustrator

0871
Designer: Tim McGrath
Client: N.M. Advertising Federation
Software/Hardware: Quark XPress, Adobe
Illustrator

Rick Rawlins/Work
0021
Art Director: Rick Rawlins
Designer: Rick Rawlins
Client: Eleven
Software/Hardware: Quark XPress, Mac
Paper/Materials: Slate

0431
Art Director: Rick Rawlins
Designer: Rick Rawlins
Client: Nathan & Bridget Rawlins
Software/Hardware: Quark XPress, Mac
Paper/Materials: Mallard Feather & Metal tin

0485
Art Director: Rick Rawlins
Designer: Rick Rawlins
Client: The Cambridge Arts Council
Software/Hardware: Quark XPress, Mac
Paper/Materials: Chipboard, Glow-in-the-Dark
Ink

0489
Art Director: Rick Rawlins
Designer: Rick Rawlins
Client: Daryl Otte
Software/Hardware: Mac, Quark XPress
Paper/Materials: Rives BFK, Apron, Glassine,
Kraft

0581
Art Director: Rick Rawlins
Designer: Rick Rawlins
Client: Eleven
Software/Hardware: Quark XPress, Mac
Paper/Materials: Bandanas, Thermo-chromatic
Bookmarks

0583
Art Director: Rick Rawlins
Designer: Rick Rawlins
Client: Cambridge Peace Commission
Software/Hardware: Quark XPress, Mac
Paper/Materials: Black board, Candle, and
Newsprint

0617
Art Director: Rick Rawlins
Designer: Rick Rawlins
Client: Art Institute of Boston
Software/Hardware: Quark XPress, Mac

0627
Art Director: Rick Rawlins
Designer: Rick Rawlins
Client: Art Institute of Boston
Software/Hardware: Quark XPress, Mac
Paper/Materials: Van Gelder, Cotton Linter

0662
Art Director: Rick Rawlins
Designer: Rick Rawlins
Client: Wellesley College
Software/Hardware: Quark XPress, Mac
Paper/Materials: Pharmaceutical Packaging,
Glassine

0718
Art Director: Rick Rawlins
Designers: Rick Rawlins, Manuel Ortega
Client: Letterpress Guild of New England
Software/Hardware: Quark XPress, Mac
Paper/Materials: Newsprint, Kraft

0771
Art Director: Rick Rawlins
Designer: Rick Rawlins
Client: The Cambridge Arts Council
Software/Hardware: Quark XPress, Mac

0794, 0837
Art Director: Rick Rawlins
Designer: Rick Rawlins
Client: Isabella Stewart Gardner Museum
Software/Hardware: Quark XPress, Mac

0917
Art Director: Rick Rawlins
Designer: Rick Rawlins
Client: Carl Tremblay
Software/Hardware: Quark XPress, Letter Press
Paper/Materials: Kraft

0955
Art Director: Rick Rawlins
Designer: Rick Rawlins
Client: Genesis
Software/Hardware: Quark XPress, Mac
Paper/Materials: Template Plastic

Rickabaugh Graphics
0226
Art Director: Eric Rickabaugh
Designer: Eric Rickabaugh
Client: Rickabaugh Graphics
Software/Hardware: Macromedia Freehand,
Mac

Riordon Design
0074
Art Director: Dan Wheaton
Designers: Shirley Riordon, Amy Montgomery
Client: In-Sync
Software/Hardware: Mac, Quark XPress,
Adobe Illustrator
Paper/Materials: Crushed Leaf & Chartham
Translucents for A-7 Envelope

0179
Art Director: Dan Wheaton
Designer: Amy Montgomery
Client: Riordon Design
Software/Hardware: Mac, Quark XPress,
Adobe Illustrator
Paper/Materials: Euroart

0201
Art Director: Dan Wheaton
Designer: Tim Warnock
Client: Riordon Design
Software/Hardware: Mac, Adobe Photoshop,
Quark XPress
Paper/Materials: Euroart, A-7 Charthem
Translucents, Envelope

0258
Art Director: Dan Wheaton
Designer: Tim Warnock
Client: X-Eye
Software/Hardware: Mac, Adobe Photoshop,
Quark XPress
Paper/Materials: Euroart

0290
Art Director: Dan Wheaton
Designers: Amy Montgomery, Sharon Pece
Client: Riordon Design
Software/Hardware: Quark XPress, Adobe
Illustrator, Adobe Photoshop
Paper/Materials: Neenah Environment

0708
Art Director: Dan Wheaton
Designer: Sharon Pece
Client: M for Men
Software/Hardware: Quark XPress
Paper/Materials: Curious Metallics, A-7
Envelope-Chartham Translucents

0819
Art Director: Dan Wheaton
Designers: Cori Hellard, Tim Warnock, Shirley
Riordon, Dan Wheaton
Client: Scotia Capital
Software/Hardware: Mac, Quark XPress,
Adobe Illustrator, Adobe Photoshop
Paper/Materials: Various Papers & Fabrics

Rob Kimmell
0849
Client: Rob Kimmell & Kristin Jensen

Robilant & Associates
0957
Art Director: Maurizio DiRobilant
Designer: Maurizio DiRobilant
Client: Self-Promotion
Paper/Materials: Aluminium Can with Olive Oil

Rome & Gold Creative
0118
Art Director: Robert E. Goldie
Designer: Lorenzo Romero
Client: Calvary of Albuquerque
Software/Hardware: Adobe Illustrator, Adobe
Photoshop

0733
Art Director: Robert E. Goldie
Designers: Lorenzo Romero, Zeke Sikelianos
Client: Tri Progress Productions
Software/Hardware: Adobe Photoshop, Adobe
Illustrator
Paper/Materials: Tickets & Envelopes, French
Paper Co. Durotone Butcher Black

Rosalia Nocerino
0517
Designer: Rosalia Nocerino
Client: Rosalia Nocerino, Frances Bonanni
Software/Hardware: Quark XPress, Mac
Paper/Materials: Cromatica (aqua), Strathmore
Elements

0546
Designer: Rosalia Nocerino
Client: Katie Couric
Software/Hardware: Quark XPress, Adobe
Illustrator, Mac
Paper/Materials: Cromatica (Yellow)

0740
Designer: Rosalia Nocerino
Client: Self
Software/Hardware: Quark XPress, Mac
Paper/Materials: Wausau Celebrations in Ivory
& Gillmore Oxford Vellium

Roundel
0260
Art Director: John Bateson
Designer: Paul Ingle
Client: Doric Signs
Software/Hardware: Mac, Quark Xpress

0462
Art Director: John Bateson
Designer: Paul Ingle
Client: Chantel Desforges
Software/Hardware: Mac, Quark XPress

0789
Art Director: John Bateson
Designer: Paul Ingle
Client: Design Business Association
Software/Hardware: Mac, Quark XPress

Paper/Materials: Chromolux Magic Lips
250gsm

Roycroft Design
0600
Art Director: Jennifer Roycroft
Designer: Jennifer Roycroft
Client: Mohawk Paper Mills
Software/Hardware: Quark XPress, Mac
Paper/Materials: Mohawk Superior

Rule 29
0157
Art Directors: Justin Ahrens, Jim Boborci
Designers: Justin Ahrens, Jim Boborci
Client: Rule 29
Software/Hardware: Quark XPress, Mac
Paper/Materials: Pegasus, Synergy

0429
Art Director: Justin Ahrens
Designer: Justin Ahrens
Software/Hardware: Quark XPress, Mac
Paper/Materials: Classic Columns, Sappi
McCoy

0456
Art Directors: Justin Ahrens, Jim Boborci
Designers: Justin Ahrens, Jim Boborci
Client: Rule 29
Software/Hardware: Quark XPress, Mac
Paper/Materials: Classic Crest

0513
Art Directors: Justin Ahrens, Jim Boborci
Designers: Justin Ahrens, Jim Boborci
Client: AIGA Chicago
Software/Hardware: Quark XPress, Mac
Paper/Materials: McCoy Uncoated

0696
Art Director: Justin Ahrens
Designer: Jessie Bultema
Client: Lighthouse Marketing
Software/Hardware: Quark XPress, Mac

0737
Art Directors: Jon McGrath, Jessie Bultema
Designers: Jon McGrath, Jessie Bultema
Software/Hardware: Quark XPress, Mac
Paper/Materials: Pegasus

0864
Art Director: Justin Ahrens
Designers: Justin Ahrens, Jon McGrath
Client: Lighthouse Marketing
Software/Hardware: Quark XPress, Mac

0949
Art Directors: Justin Ahrens, Jim Boborci
Designers: Justin Ahrens, Jim Boborci
Client: Rule 29
Software/Hardware: Quark XPress, Mac
Paper/Materials: Pegasus, Synergy

0999
Art Directors: Justin Ahrens, Jim Boborci
Designers: Justin Ahrens, Jim Boborci
Client: Ascentives
Software/Hardware: Quark XPress, Mac
Paper/Materials: Classic Crest

Russell Design
0597
Art Director: Tina Winey
Designer: Laura Ploszaj
Client: City Harvest
Software/Hardware: Adobe Illustrator, Quark
XPress
Paper/Materials: Mohawk Superfine

0651
Designer: Dana Snider
Client: Amanda Allen
Software/Hardware: Quark XPress, Adobe
Illustrator, Mac

0803
Art Director: Tina Winey
Designer: Laura Ploszaj
Client: City Harvest
Software/Hardware: Quark XPress
Paper/Materials: Envelope-Evanescent,
Invitation-Superfine

0816
Designer: Dana Snider
Client: Stephanie Obando
Software/Hardware: Quark XPress, Adobe
Illustrator, Mac

0892
Art Director: Tony Russell
Designer: Julie Beard
Client: Russell Design
Software/Hardware: Quark Xpress

0952
Art Director: Tony Russell
Designer: Julie Beard
Client: Nasdaq
Software/Hardware: Quark Xpress

Ruth Hulmerind
0944
Art Director: Ruth Hulmerind
Designer: Juri Loun
Client: Ruth Hulmerind
Software/Hardware: Macromedia Flash 9.0
Paper/Materials: Countryside Mishal

0963
Art Director: Ruth Hulmerind
Designer: Juri Loun
Client: Modo Paper
Software/Hardware: Macromedia Flash 9.0
Paper/Materials: Retreeve Earthtints, Invercote

0977
Art Director: Ruth Hulmerind
Designer: Juri Kass
Client: Modo Paper
Software/Hardware: Macromedia Freehand .0
Paper/Materials: Invercote

0981
Art Director: Ruth Hulmerind
Designer: Juri Loun
Client: MAP Eesti
Software/Hardware: Macromedia Freehand 9.0
Paper/Materials: Evanescent, Invercote, Creato

S

Sagmeister, Inc
0580
Art Director: Stefan Sagmeister
Designer: Hjalti Karlsson
Client: Sagmeister, Inc
Software/Hardware: Adobe Illustrator, Mac
Paper/Materials: Fart Cushion

0714
Art Director: Stefan Sagmeister
Designer: Matthias Arnstberger
Client: Sagmeister
Software/Hardware: Adobe Photoshop, Mac
Paper/Materials: 300 gsm Board

Samata Mason
0877
Art Director: Pat Samata
Designer: Lynne Nagel
Client: Fine Arts Engraving
Software/Hardware: Quark XPress, Adobe
Photoshop, Mac
Paper/Materials: Classic Crest 100#, Cover &
Text Avalanche White Smooth

Sayles Graphic Design

0103
Art Director: John Sayles
Designers: John Sayles, Som Inthalangsy
Client: Ahmanson Family
Software/Hardware: Adobe Illustrator
Paper/Materials: Cougar Natural 100# Cover

0532
Art Director: John Sayles
Designers: John Sayles, Som Inthalangsy
Client: American Institute of Architects
Software/Hardware: Adobe Illustrator, Quark XPress
Paper/Materials: Mohawk Navajo 80# Cover, Text

0569
Art Director: John Sayles
Designers: John Sayles, Som Inthalangsy
Client: City of Ankeny, Iowa
Software/Hardware: Adobe Illustrator, Quark XPress
Paper/Materials: Cougar 803 Cover Screenprinted on Corrugated Box

0608
Art Director: John Sayles
Designers: John Sayles, Som Inthalangsy
Client: Hewitt Associates
Software/Hardware: Adobe Illustrator
Paper/Materials: Luna Matte 80# Cover

0817
Art Director: John Sayles
Designers: John Sayles, Som Inthalangsy
Client: Art Fights Back
Software/Hardware: Adobe Illustrator
Paper/Materials: Mohawk Navajo 80# Cover

0868
Art Director: John Sayles
Designers: John Sayles, Som Inthalangsy
Client: Proctor Mechanical
Software/Hardware: Adobe Illustrator, Quark XPress
Paper/Materials: Luna Matte 60# on Corrugated Box

0898
Art Director: John Sayles
Designers: John Sayles, Som Inthalangsy
Client: United Way
Software/Hardware: Adobe Illustrator, Quark XPress
Paper/Materials: Cougar 80# Cover Screenprinted on Corrugated Box

0912
Art Director: John Sayles
Designers: John Sayles, Som Inthalangsy
Client: Brix
Software/Hardware: Adobe Illustrator
Paper/Materials: Cougar 100# Cover

0975
Art Director: John Sayles
Designers: John Sayles, Som Inthalangsy
Client: Sbemco International
Software/Hardware: Adobe Illustrator, Quark XPress
Paper/Materials: Luna Matte 80# Cover

0980
Art Director: John Sayles
Designers: John Sayles, Som Inthalangsy
Client: Official Airline Guide (OAG)
Software/Hardware: Adobe Illustrator, Quark XPress
Paper/Materials: Cougar Natural 80# Cover

Sayre Gaydos
0095, 0122, 0123, 0169, 0171,0172, 0174, 0187, 0189, 0200, 0210, 0255
Designer: Sayre Gaydos
Client: Ink Farm

0100, 0195
Designer: Sayre Gaydos
Client: Peter Kruty Edition

0523
Designer: Sayre Gaydos
Client: Dadourian & Nelson

0731
Designer: Sayre Gaydos
Client: Kristin Newman Designs

0753
Designer: Sayre Gaydos
Client: Leigh Merinoff

0899
Designer: Sayre Gaydos
Art Director: Stephanie Brody-Lederman
Client: Stephanie Brody-Lederman

Scott Baldwin
0024, 0026, 0030
Designer: Scott Baldwin
Client: Ironworks Graphic Sign
Software/Hardware: Linocut, Letterpress
Paper/Materials: Exact Matte Cover

0027
Designer: Scott Baldwin
Client: ironworksgraphics.com
Software/Hardware: Linocut, Letterpress
Paper/Materials: Exact Matte Cove

0085
Designer: Scott Baldwin
Client: Scott Baldwin
Software/Hardware: Linocut, Adobe Photoshop

Selbert Perkins Design
0453
Art Director: Clifford Selbert
Designer: Avvi Raquel-Santos
Client: Selbert Perkins Design
Software/Hardware: Adobe Illustrator, Mac
Paper/Materials: Cardboard

0658
Art Director: Sheri Bates
Client: Citizen Schools
Software/Hardware: Quark XPress, Mac
Paper/Materials: Monadnock

0680
Art Directors: Robin Perkins, Clifford Selbert
Designer: Erin Carney
Client: Elizabeth Sachs
Software/Hardware: Mac OS, Adobe Illustrator

0904
Art Directors: Robin Perkins, Clifford Selbert
Designer: Jessica Bittani
Client: Self Promotion
Software/Hardware: Mac OS, Adobe Illustrator, Adobe Photoshop, Quark Xpress

0923
Art Directors: Robin Perkins, Clifford Selbert
Designer: Ross Geerdes
Client: Anti Gravity
Software/Hardware: Mac OS 9

Shamlian Advertising
0001
Art Director: Fred Shamlian
Designer: Fred Shamlian
Client: Self-Promo
Software/Hardware: Quark XPress, Adobe Illustrator
Paper/Materials: CD/Claimsbell

0036
Art Director: Fred Shamlian
Designer: Jessica Paolella
Client: The Vague Family
Software/Hardware: Quark XPress, Adobe Illustrator, Adobe Photoshop
Paper/Materials: Paper, CD, Triangle

Shea, Inc.
0340
Art Director: James Rahn
Designer: James Rahn
Client: Shea, Inc.
Software/Hardware: Adobe Illustrator
Paper/Materials: Curious Metallic

Sibley Peteet Design-Dallas
0192
Art Director: Don Gibley
Designer: Brandon Kirk
Client: Sibley Peteet Design-Dallas
Software/Hardware: Adobe Illustrator, Photoshop
Paper/Materials: French Construction, Pure white

0193
Art Director: Don Sibley
Designer: Brandon Kirk
Client: Sibley Peteet Design-Dallas
Software/Hardware: Adobe Illustrator, Adobe Photoshop, Streamline
Paper/Materials: Mohawk Supreme

0447
Designer: Brandon Kirk
Client: Brandon Kirk, Julia Holcomb
Software/Hardware: Adobe Illustrator, Quark XPress
Paper/Materials: French Speckle Tone

Simon Does
0188
Art Director: Karen Simon
Designer: Karen Simon
Client: Simon Does
Software/Hardware: Max, Quark XPress, Adobe Illustrator

Simply Put Design
0530
Art Director: Carrene Tracy
Client: Margaret Jacobi
Software/Hardware: Adobe Photoshop, Adobe Illustrator
Paper/Materials: Ribbon

0704, 0768
Art Director: Carrene Tracy
Software/Hardware: Adobe Illustrator
Paper/Materials: Strathmore Pastelle

0751
Art Director: Carrene Tracy
Client: Louise Kangas
Software/Hardware: Adobe Illustrator,
Adobe Photoshop
Paper/Materials: Mohawk Superfine

0782
Art Director: Carrene Tracy
Software/Hardware: Adobe Illustrator
Paper/Materials: Mohawk Superfine

SiSu Design
0604
Art Director: Jennifer Stucker
Designer: Jennifer Stucker
Client: Josh & Tonya Alkire
Software/Hardware: Macromedia Freehand

0624
Art Director: Jennifer Stucker
Designer: Jennifer Stucker
Client: Boys & Girls Clubs of Toledo
Software/Hardware: Macromedia Freehand
Paper/Materials: Lustro

SK Visual
0133
Art Directors: Katya Lyumkis, Spencer Lum
Designers: Katya Lyumkis, Spencer Lum
Client: Self-Promotion
Software/Hardware: Adobe Illustrator,
Paper/Materials: Styrofoam Trays, Tin Cans,
Cellophane Wrap, Plastic Shreds & Tea

Sky Design
0919
Art Director: W. Todd Vaught
Designer: Carrie Wallace
Client: Sky Design
Software/Hardware: Adobe Illustrator 8.0
Paper/Materials: Stamped Aluminum Coated
Paper

Smudge Ink
0173
Designer: Kate Saliba
Paper/Materials: White Cotton Paper

0183
Client: Kate Saliba
Paper/Materials: Rives BFK Tan Paper, Hand-
Carved Linoleum Block

0253, 0256, 0259, 0331, 0332, 0333
Client: Kate Saliba

0281
Designer: Kate Saliba
Client: Private
Paper/Materials: 600 gr. Copper Plate, Bright
White Paper

0418
Designer: Kate Saliba
Client: Private
Paper/Materials: Magnani Pescia Italian Blue
paper

0439
Designer: Kate Saliba
Client: Private
Paper/Materials: Lenox 100% Cotton Paper

0464
Designer: Kate Saliba
Client: Private
Paper/Materials: 100% Cotton Paper

0829
Designer: Kate Saliba
Client: Private
Software/Hardware: Sewing Machine, Chandler
& Price Letterpress
Paper/Materials: 100% Cotton Lenox White
Paper

Sommese Design
0457, 0982, 0995
Art Directors: Lanny Sommese, Kristin
Sommese
Designer: Lanny Sommese
Client: Sommese Design
Software/Hardware: Adobe Illustrator, Adobe
Photoshop, Mac

0681
Art Directors: Kristin Sommese, Lanny
Sommese
Client: Sommese Design
Software/Hardware: Mac, Adobe Illustrator,
Adobe Photoshop
Paper/Materials: Dancing Forks

Sonsoles Llorens Design
0016
Art Director: Sonsoles Llorens
Designer: Sonsoles Llorens
Client: Sonsoles Llorens Design
Software/Hardware: Macromedia Freehand,
Mac
Paper/Materials: Offset Printing

0244
Art Director: Sonsoles Llorens
Designer: Sonsoles Llorens
Client: Sonsoles Llorens
Software/Hardware: Macromedia Freehand,
Mac
Paper/Materials: Plastic Ball, Silkscreening,
Paper

Special Modern Design
0534
Art Director: Karen Barranco
Designer: Karen Barranco
Client: Sitton Tayler
Software/Hardware: Mac, Adobe Illustrator,
Adobe Photoshop
Paper/Materials: Bark, Tissue, Ribbon,
Offset Printing

Splash Interactive
0151
Art Director: Ivy Wong
Designer: Ivy Wong
Client: Splash Interactive
Software/Hardware: Adobe Illustrator, Adobe
Photoshop, Mac G4

Stacey Bakaj
0219, 0878
Designer: Stacey Bakaj
Client: Stacey Bakaj
Software/Hardware: Vandercook SP15
Paper/Materials: Letterpress

Stahl Partners, Inc.
0885
Art Director: David Stahl
Client: Stahl Design Inc.
Software/Hardware: Quark XPress,
Paper/Materials: French Paper Duro-Tone,
Butcher Off-White

Steff Geissbuhler (Chermayeff & Geismar, Inc.)
0015
Art Director: Steff Geissbuhler
Designer: Steff Geissbuhler
Client: Schneiderman/Geissbuhler
Paper/Materials: Reich Paper, Iridescent Offset
& Engraving

0017
Art Director: Steff Geissbuhler
Designer: Steff Geissbuhler
Client: Schneiderman/Geissbuhler
Paper/Materials: Strathmore papers, Die-Cut
& Engraving

0223
Art Director: Steff Geissbuhler
Designer: Steff Geissbuhler
Client: Schneiderman/Geissbuhler
Paper/Materials: Strathmore paper, Blind
Emboss & Engraving

Stephen Burdick Design
0985
Designer: Stephen Burdick
Client: Self-Promotion
Software/Hardware: Adobe Photoshop
Paper/Materials: Inkjet Output

Stereobloc
0639, 0640
Art Director: Holger Stumpe
Designer: Maik Brummundt
Client: Galerie Griedervonpotikamer
Software/Hardware: Quark XPress
Paper/Materials: Profisilk 350 gm 3

0966
Art Director: Udo Albrecht
Designer: Maik Brummundt
Client: Stereobloc
Software/Hardware: Adobe Photoshop, Quark
XPress
Paper/Materials: Cromolux

0970
Art Director: Udo Albrecht
Designer: Udo Albrecht
Client: Stereobloc
Software/Hardware: Adobe Photoshop, Quark
XPress
Paper/Materials: Invercote, Albato 290gm 3

Studio International
0888, 0902
Art Director: Boris Liubicic
Designer: Boris Liubicic
Client: Europe 2020/Minitry RH
Software/Hardware: Corel Draw
Paper/Materials: B/W Dacot 200/g

Studio J
0247
Designer: Angela Jackson
Client: Angela Jackson
Software/Hardware: Adobe Illustrator
Paper/Materials: Spice Jars, Digital Color
Copies

0991
Designer: Angela Jackson
Client: Angela Jackson, Studio J
Software/Hardware: Mac, Adobe Illustrator
Paper/Materials: Digital Copies, Homemade
Candy

Stults Printing Co.
0922
Art Director: Rachel Stults
Designer: Rachel Stults

Sudduth Dsign Co.
0139
Art Director: Toby Sudduth
Designer: Toby Sudduth
Client: Personal
Software/Hardware: Adobe Illustrator, Adobe
Photoshop
Paper/Materials: Epson Inkjet

0460
Art Directors: Holly & Toby Sudduth
Designer: Toby Sudduth
Client: Holly & Toby Sudduth
Software/Hardware: Adobe Illustrator
Paper/Materials: 2 Color Letterpress with
Various Photographs

Swirly Designs by Lianne & Paul
0053
Art Director: Lianne Stoddard
Client: Swirly Designs
Software/Hardware: Adobe Illustrator 8.0, Mac
Paper/Materials: Celery Color Cover Stock &
Pink Glitter

0267
Art Director: Lianne Stoddard
Designer: Paul Stoddard
Client: Swirly Designs
Software/Hardware: Adobe Illustrator 8.0, Mac
Paper/Materials: White Texture Cover Stock,
Orange Vellum & Eyelets

t

That's Nice, LLC
0057
Art Director: Nigel Walker
Designer: Erica Heitman
Client: That's Nice LLC
Software/Hardware: Quark XPress, Adobe
Illustrator, Adobe Photoshop

0190
Art Director: Nigel Walker
Designer: Phil Evans
Client: That's Nice, LLC
Software/Hardware: Quark XPress, Adobe
Illustrator, Adobe Photoshop

0876
Art Director: Nigel Walker
Designers: David Phan, Scott Robertson, Elan
Harris
Client: That's Nice, LLC
Software/Hardware: Quark XPress, Adobe
Illustrator, Adobe Photoshop

0887
Art Director: Nigel Walker
Designer: Kaoru Kaojima
Client: That's Nice, LLC
Software/Hardware: Quark XPress, Adobe
Illustrator, Adobe Photoshop

0964
Art Director: Nigel Walker
Designers: Erica Heitman, Scott Robertson
Client: That's Nice, LLC
Software/Hardware: Quark XPress, Adobe
Illustrator, Adobe Photoshop

The Commissary
0664
Art Director: Lucas Charles
Designer: Alison Charles
Client: Singelyn Family
Software/Hardware: Quark XPress, Mac
Paper/Materials: 80lb Strathmore

0688
Art Director: Lucas Charles
Designer: Alison Charles
Client: Armstrong & Fox Family
Software/Hardware: Quark XPress, Adobe
Illustrator, Mac
Paper/Materials: 60lb Strathmore

0717
Art Director: Lucas Charles
Designer: Lucas Charles
Client: The University of Memphis
Software/Hardware: Adobe Illustrator, Mac
Paper/Materials: Glassine Envelope, 60 lb.
Uncoated

0833
Art Director: Lucas Charles
Designer: Lucas Charles
Client: The Charles & Johnson Family
Software/Hardware: Quark XPress, Adobe
Photoshop, Mac
Paper/Materials: 60lb Strathmore

0841
Art Director: Lucas Charles
Designer: Alison Charles
Client: Hall & Wilson Family
Software/Hardware: Adobe Photoshop, Quark
XPress, Mac
Paper/Materials: French Paper

0848
Art Director: Lucas Charles
Designer: Hudd Byard
Client: Hinshaw & Byard Families
Software/Hardware: Adobe Photoshop, Quark
XPress, Mac
Paper/Materials: Glassine Envelopes, Wausau
Bristol

The Point, LLC
0798
Art Director: Janet Fried
Designer: Janet Fried
Client: Memorial Art Gallery
Software/Hardware: Quark XPress, Mac

0896
Art Director: Janet Fried
Designer: Janet Fried
Client: Syracuse University
Software/Hardware: Quark XPress, Mac

The Post Press
0362, 0373
Art Director: Martha Carothers
Designer: Martha Carothers
Client: The Post Press
Paper/Materials: Rubber Stamp, Hole Punch

Timespin
0317
Designer: Tino Schmidt
Client: Timespin
Software/Hardware: Macromedia Freehand,
Mac
Paper/Materials: 250g Special Paper, Opaque
Envelope

Tom Fowler, Inc.
0069
Art Director: Brien O'Reilly
Designer: Brien O'Reilly
Client: Brien & Sandi O'Reilly
Software/Hardware: Quark XPress, Adobe
Photoshop
Paper/Materials: Hammermill Laserprint

0430
Art Directors: Brien & Sandi O'Reilly
Designer: Brien O'Reilly
Client: Brien & Sandi O'Reilly
Software/Hardware: Quark XPress, Adobe
Photoshop
Paper/Materials: Mohawk Superfine

0614
Art Director: Tom G. Fowler
Designers: Thomas G. Fowler, Karl S.
Maruyama
Client: Pfizer, Inc.
Software/Hardware: Adobe Illustrator
Paper/Materials: Magic Cube, Pfizer Holiday
Cube

Tong Design Graphic Studio
0002, 0116, 0346
Art Director: Tong Wai Hang
Designer: Tong Wai Hang
Client: Tong Design Graphic Studio
Software/Hardware: Adobe Illustrator 8.0

Top Design Studio
0154
Art Director: Peleg Top
Designer: Peleg Top
Client: Quincy Jones Music Publishing

0348
Art Director: Peleg Top
Designer: Peleg Top
Client: Top Design Studio

0509
Art Director: Peleg Top
Designer: Peleg Top
Client: Crystal Stairs

0563
Art Director: Peleg Top
Designer: Peleg Top
Client: Technicolor Digital Cineman

0596
Art Director: Peleg Top
Designers: Peleg Top/Rebekah Beaton
Client: City of Hope/NCFDIC

0786
Art Director: Peleg Top
Designer: Peleg Top
Client: City of Hope

Towers Perrin
0010
Art Director: Michelle Goodman
Designer: Lavonne Czech
Client: Towers Perrin
Software/Hardware: Mac
Paper/Materials: Beckett, Classic Crest
Illustration: Carolyn Williams

0067
Art Directors: Fawn Roth Winick, Scott May
Designer: Media Consultants
Client: Towers Perrin
Software/Hardware: Mac, Quark XPress,
Adobe Photoshop, Adobe Illustrator
Paper/Materials: White McCoy Dull Cover
Vellum

Tracy Design
0038
Art Director: Jan Tracy
Designers: Rachel Karaca, Sarah Bray
Client: Tracy Design
Software/Hardware: Adobe Illustrator, Mac
Paper/Materials: French Speckle Tone Tin
Cans

Transcend
0224
Art Director: Hung Q. Tran
Designer: Hung Q. Tran
Client: Allison Donahue
Software/Hardware: Adobe Photoshop, Quark
Xpress

0676
Art Director: Hung Q. Tran
Designer: Hung Q. Tran
Client: Transcend
Software/Hardware: Adobe Photoshop, Quark
XPress

Triana The
0476
Designer: Triana The
Software/Hardware: Macromedia Freehand
Paper/Materials: Paper Bags

Trudy Cole-Zielanski Design
0948
Art Director: Trudy Cole-Zielanski
Designer: Trudy Cole-Zielanski
Client: Trudy Cole-Zielanski Design
Software/Hardware: Adobe Illustrator, Mac

Turner Duckworth
0938
Art Directors: Bruce Duckworth, David Turner
Designer: Mark Waters
Client: Turner Duckworth
Paper/Materials: Various

U

University of San Diego
0634
Art Director: Barbara Ferguson
Designer: Barbara Ferguson
Client: Office of Alumni Relations
Software/Hardware: Quark XPress, Adobe
Photoshop, Adobe Illustrator

UP Creative Design & Advertising Co.
0042
Art Director: Jenny Pai
Designer: Jenny Pai
Client: UP Creative Design & Advertising
Software/Hardware: Adobe Illustrator, Mac
Paper/Materials: Paper

0119
Art Director: Andy Lee
Designer: Peter Lee
Client: Shin Yeh Restaurant
Software/Hardware: Adobe Illustrator, Mac
Paper/Materials: Paper

0304
Designer: Javen Lin
Client: Chunghwa Post
Software/Hardware: Adobe Illustrator, Mac
Paper/Materials: Paper

0480
Designer: Javen Lin
Client: Javen Lin
Software/Hardware: Adobe Illustrator, Mac
Paper/Materials: Paper

0657
Art Director: Andy Lee
Designer: Andy Lee
Client: Jeff Tung
Software/Hardware: Adobe Illustrator, Mac
Paper/Materials: Paper & Chinese Know

0674
Art Director: Ben Wang
Designer: Ben Wang
Client: Ben Wang
Software/Hardware: Adobe Illustrator, Mac
Paper/Materials: Paper & Silk

0862
Art Director: Ben Wang
Designer: Ben Wang
Client: Jeffrey Wu
Software/Hardware: Adobe Illustrator, Mac
Paper/Materials: Paper

Uturn Design
0495, 0555, 0588
Art Director: Stephanie Zelman
Client: Boston Public Library Foundation

0551
Art Director: Stephanie Zelman
Client: Karen & Adam Tager

0552, 0732
Art Director: Stephanie Zelman
Client: Boston Stock Exchange

V

Vestigio
0217, 0567
Art Director: Emanuel Barbosa
Designer: Emanual Barbosa
Client: CD.Rom Jeans
Software/Hardware: Macromedia Freehand,
Mac
Paper/Materials: Torras Paper

0668
Art Director: Emanuel Barbosa
Designer: Emanual Barbosa
Client: Mantra Discotheque
Software/Hardware: Mac, Macromedia
Freehand, Adobe Photoshop
Paper/Materials: Torras

Viñas Design
0018, 0425, 0443, 0790, 0845
Art Director: Jaime Viñas
Designer: Jaime Viñas

Visual Dialogue
0776
Art Director: Fritz Klaetke
Designer: Fritz Klaetke
Client: Isabella Stewart Gardner Museum
Software/Hardware: Quark XPress
Paper/Materials: Cougar Opaque

0865
Art Director: Fritz Klaetke
Designer: Fritz Klaetke
Client: AIGA Boston
Software/Hardware: Quark XPress, Adobe
Photoshop
Paper/Materials: Black Marker, Curious
Metallics, Utopia Onex

Visual Solutions
0228
Art Director: Cynthia Anderson
Designer: Cynthia Anderson
Software/Hardware: Quark XPress
Paper/Materials: Curious Paper, Metallic, Light
Specs, Glue, Glitter

Voice
0054
Art Director: Scott Carslake
Designer: Scott Carslake
Client: Voice
Software/Hardware: Adobe Photoshop, Mac
Paper/Materials: Tablex, Ink Marker

Vrontikis Design Office
0343, 0937
Art Director: Petrula Vrontikis
Designers: Various
Client: Vrontikis Design Office
Software/Hardware: Various
Paper/Materials: Various

0686
Art Director: Petrula Vrontikis
Designer: Tammy Kim
Client: Global-Dining, Inc.
Software/Hardware: Adobe Illustrator, Mac
Paper/Materials: Various

0826
Art Director: Petrula Vrontikis
Designer: Kim Sage
Client: Global-Dining, Inc.
Software/Hardware: Adobe Illustrator, Mac
Paper/Materials: Various

W

W.C. Burgard Illustration
0158, 0170, 0379
Art Director: W.C. Burgard
Designer: W.C Burgard
Client: W.C. Burgard Xmas Card
Paper/Materials: Acrylic, Collage

0315
Art Director: W.C. Burgard
Designer: W.C. Burgard
Client: W.C. Burgard Xmas Card
Paper/Materials: Pencil, Zipatone

0380
Art Director: W.C. Burgard
Designer: W.C. Burgard
Client: W.C. Burgard Xmas Card
Paper/Materials: Pastel, Collage

Wages Design, Inc.
0595
Art Director: Bob Wages
Designer: Joanna Tak
Client: Antron
Software/Hardware: Adobe Photoshop, Adobe
Illustrator, Mac
Paper/Materials: Domtar Sandpiper

0703
Art Director: Bob Wages
Designer: Diane Kim
Client: Antron
Software/Hardware: Adobe Photoshop, Adobe
Illustrator, Mac
Paper/Materials: Neenah Classic Crest

0809
Art Director: Bob Wages
Designer: Matthew Taylor
Client: Antron
Software/Hardware: Adobe Illustrator, Mac
Paper/Materials: Printer Stock

0863
Art Director: Bob Wages
Designer: Joanna Tak
Client: Antron
Software/Hardware: Adobe Photoshop, Adobe
Illustrator, Mac
Paper/Materials: Neenah Classic Crest

Wallace Church
0197
Art Director: Stan Church
Designer: Stan Church
Client: Stan Church
Software/Hardware: Adobe Illustrator 8.0
Paper/Materials: Classic Crest Paper

0288
Art Director: Stan Church
Designer: Stan Church
Client: Wallace Church, Inc
Software/Hardware: Adobe Illustrator, Mac
Paper/Materials: K. Grafx Printing &
Embossing

0465
Art Director: Stan Church
Designer: Stan Church
Client: Wallace Church, Inc.
Software/Hardware: Adobe Illustrator, Mac
Paper/Materials: Classic Crest Paper

0503
Art Director: Stan Church
Designer: Laurence Haggerty
Client: Wallace Church, Inc
Software/Hardware: Adobe Illustrator, Mac,
Paper/Materials: Chinet paper Plates with
Rubber Stamp

0785
Art Director: John Bruno
Designers: Clare Reece, Ray Bould
Client: Wallace Church Inc
Software/Hardware: Adobe Illustrator, Mac
Paper/Materials: Kraft Paper, Fortune Telling
Fish, Black Linen Envelope

0936
Art Directors: John Bruno, Laurence Haggerty
Designer: Laurence Haggerty
Client: Wallace Church, Inc.
Software/Hardware: Adobe Illustrator 8, Mac
Paper/Materials: Plastic Shrink Wrap, Baseball
Stitch with Red Cotton Thread, CD w/ Baseball
Music

0989
Art Director: Stan Church
Designer: John Bruno
Client: Wallace Church, Inc.
Software/Hardware: Adobe Illustrator 8.0, Mac
Paper/Materials: Wine Bottle, Turkey Poppers
& Label

Watts Design
0663
Art Director: Peter Watts
Designer: Peter Watts
Client: Australian Cricket Board

Webber Design Werks
0410
Art Director: Sean Webber
Designer: Sean Webber
Client: The Webber Family
Software/Hardware: Adobe Photoshop, Quark
XPress
Paper/Materials: Neenah, Classic Columns,
Indigo 80# Cover, Hammermill 24# Text

Whitenoise
0191
Art Director: Mark Case
Designer: Juue Turkington
Client: Whitenoise
Software/Hardware: Adobe Illustrator
Paper/Materials: 350 gsm Matt Art Card

White Rhino
0327
Art Director: Dan Greenwald
Designer: Athena Hermann
Client: White Rhino
Software/Hardware: Mac, Quark XPress
Paper/Materials: French Frostone

0667
Creative Director: Dan Greenwald
Designer: Athena Herrmann
Client: Foundry Sports Medicine and Fitness
Software/Hardware: Mac, Adobe Illustrator,
Quark XPress, Adobe Photoshop
Paper/Materials: Benefit, Living Tree, French
Carnival

Wing Chan Design
0926
Art Director: Wing Chan
Designers: Wing Chan, Eric Chan, Ryoichi
Yamazaki, Yee-Hwa Kim
Client: Wing Chan Design
Software/Hardware: Quark XPress, Adobe
Photoshop
Paper/Materials: Zanders mega Dull, 100#
Cover

Wilson Harvey
0047
Art Director: Paul Burgess
Designers: Paul Burgess, Peter Usher
Client: Chameleon
Software/Hardware: Mac, Quark XPress,
Adobe Illustrator, Adobe Photoshop

0177, 0515
Art Director: Paul Burgess
Designer: Wai Lau
Client: Wilson Harvey
Software/Hardware: Mac, Quark XPress,
Adobe Illustrator, Adobe Photoshop

0442
Art Director: Paul Burgess
Designer: Ben Wood
Client: Charlie & Kate Hoult
Software/Hardware: Mac, Quark XPress,
Adobe Illustrator, Adobe Photoshop

0475
Art Director: Paul Burgess
Designers: Paul Burgess, Richard Baker
Client: Paul Henerdine
Software/Hardware: Mac, Quark XPress,
Adobe Illustrator, Adobe Photoshop

0832
Art Director: Paul Burgess
Designer: Paul Burgess
Client: Kirstin, Paul, Teg
Software/Hardware: Mac, Quark XPress,
Adobe Illustrator, Adobe Photoshop

y

Yee Design
0208
Art Director: Danny Yee
Designers: Danny Yee, Sue Yee
Client: Yee Design
Software/Hardware: Adobe Illustrator
Paper/Materials: Tin

Yee-Ping Cho Design
0113
Designer: Yee-Ping Cho
Client: Delta Graphics
Paper/Materials: C1S Card

0155
Designer: Yee-Ping Cho
Client: Aardvark/Syndicate Press
Software/Hardware: Letterpress
Paper/Materials: Lana Watercolor 100% Cotton

0825
Designer: Yee-Ping Cho
Client: Technicolor
Software/Hardware: Adobe Illustrator, Mac
Paper/Materials: Neenah Classic Crest

0853
Designer: Yee-Ping Cho
Client: Patti Correll
Software/Hardware: Mac, Adobe Photoshop,
Adobe Illustrator
Paper/Materials: Epson

Z

Zappata Disenadores S.C.
0571
Art Director: Ibo Angulo
Designer: Ibo Angulo
Client: Grupo Expansion (Elle Magazine)
Software/Hardware: Macromedia Freehand,
Adobe Photoshop
Paper/Materials: Couche

0747
Art Director: Ibo Angulo
Designer: Ibo Angulo
Client: Claudine & Holger Stamm
Software/Hardware: Macromedia Freehand
8.0, Adobe Photoshop
Paper/Materials: Recycled Paper, Albanene,
Cord

0932
Art Director: Ibo Angulo
Designer: Ibo Angulo
Client: Laura Lavalle
Software/Hardware: Macromedia Freehand 8,
Adobe Photoshop
Paper/Materials: Couche

Zeroart Studio
0741
Art Directors: Jo Lo, Loy Yu Hin
Designers: Jo Lo & Nicole Chu
Client: Self Promotion (Wedding Card)
Software/Hardware: Macromedia Freehand,
Mac
Paper/Materials: Card-2/0 grm Art Paper,
Process Color & Material Color Envelope-
100grm White Woodfree Paper, Pantone Color

ZGraphics, Ltd.
0058, 0394
Art Director: LouAnn Zeller
Designer: Kris Martinez Farrell
Client: Contempo Design
Software/Hardware: Quark XPress, Adobe
Photoshop, Mac
Paper/Materials: Curious Iridescents, Neenah
Classic Crest

0090
Art Director: LouAnn Zeller
Designer: Kris Martinez Farrell
Client: ZGraphics, Ltd
Software/Hardware: Quark Xpress, Adobe
Photoshop
Paper/Materials: CTI Papers, Constellation
Jade Raster, Neenah Classic Crest, Super
Smooth

0522
Art Director: LouAnn Zeller
Designer: Renee Clark
Client: One Small Voice Foundation
Software/Hardware: Quark XPress, Adobe
Photoshop, Mac
Paper/Materials: Winner Gloss

0536
Art Director: LouAnn Zeller
Designer: Renee Clark
Client: Studio C.
Software/Hardware: Quark XPress, Adobe
Photoshop, Mac
Paper/Materials: Fraser Genesis CTI Papers
Glama

0984
Art Director: LouAnn Zeller
Designer: Renee Clark
Client: ZGraphics, Ltd.
Software/Hardware: Quark XPress, Adobe
Illustrator, Mac
Paper/Materials: Appleton Utopia Premium

ABOUT THE AUTHOR

Peter King & Company has been developing carefully crafted, concept-driven design for corporate, nonprofit, and individual clients since 1994. The studio's focus on fresh, cost-effective solutions has enabled Peter King & Company to satisfy the communications needs of a wide range of organizations, from global corporations to foundations to entrepreneurial firms.

The studio's services include corporate identity development, web and print communications, book design, packaging, trade show and event design, copywriting, account management services, and print production managment. Peter King & Company is located in Boston's Fort Point area.

To learn more, please visit www.peterkingandcompany.com